CW01652126

LEARN TO TYPE IN THIRTY DAYS

A Home-Study Course

SECOND EDITION

MANUAL · ELECTRIC · ELECTRONIC

Brenda Beaver

NOTE: The designations, names, telephone numbers and addresses used in the exercises contained in this book are intended to be fictitious.

First Edition Published 1984 by B.Beaver, Porchfield, I.O.W.
Reprinted 1985, 1986, 1987 & 1988
SECOND EDITION PUBLISHED 1989 by B.Beaver, Coombe Bissett, Salisbury, Wilts.
Reprinted 1990, 1991, 1992, 1993, 1994, 1995, 1996, 1997 & 1998

Printed by *Offset Colour Print*, Southampton (01703) 632111

ISBN 0 9509666 1 4

INTRODUCTION

Learn to Type in Thirty Days (A Home-Study Course) is for the beginner or two-finger typist who wishes to become a skilled touch-typist in the minimum amount of time and for those who wish to improve on their present ability.

In preparing this book, consideration has been given to the personal typing needs of everyone including the student, creative writer, teacher and committee member.

The first section is divided into thirty lessons giving easy to follow step-by-step instructions – each lesson should take approximately one hour to complete. For best results, one hour per day for thirty days should be spent in serious practice in the kind of atmosphere that you find conducive to learning. During the first week you may prefer to divide the lessons into two half-hour sessions each day.

From experience gained in class-room teaching, I know that the beginner needs constant reminders of the techniques essential to good touch-typing in order to prevent bad habits being formed. I have therefore included in the initial lessons, reminders on the do's and don't's of typewriting, as well as remedies for the problems you may experience.

The keys are introduced in an order that immediately permits the typing of words and prose – no time is spent on typing difficult combinations of characters that do not occur in the English language. At the end of the second day's practice, you should be able to type with ease the phrases given at the end of Lesson 2 and begin to feel a sense of achievement which will spur you on to the next lesson and the next. The skill of typewriting, like any other skill, cannot be gained without effort and practice, but once you have become an efficient typist I am sure you will feel that the effort was well worth-while.

The second section of the book contains information, samples and exercises on business documents, literary work, etc. and is intended for those who wish to continue to build on their newly acquired skill by selecting and typing the exercises appropriate to the area in which they wish to specialize.

I am sure that if you accept the challenge and follow this scheme of work, you will very soon be able to type, with confidence and pleasure, any piece of work you create, whether it is a personal letter or an essay. You will also be happy in the knowledge that you have acquired not only a skill but an art.

BRENDA BEAVER

CONTENTS

BEFORE YOU TYPE

check . . .

POSITION OF:

PAPER – Straight; inserted at '0' on Paper Scale
PAPER BAIL AND ROLLERS – Placed firmly on paper
MARGIN STOPS – Correctly set for specific exercise
LINE-SPACE REGULATOR – In selected position
MACHINE – Front of frame in line with edge of desk/table
BOOK – At right

Correct Posture

FEET – Apart; flat on floor
BODY – Centred on 'J'; a handspan from machine
BACK – Straight; body **slightly** forward from hips
WAIST – Supported by back of chair or cushion
SHOULDERS – Back but relaxed

Curve of hand – **Manual**

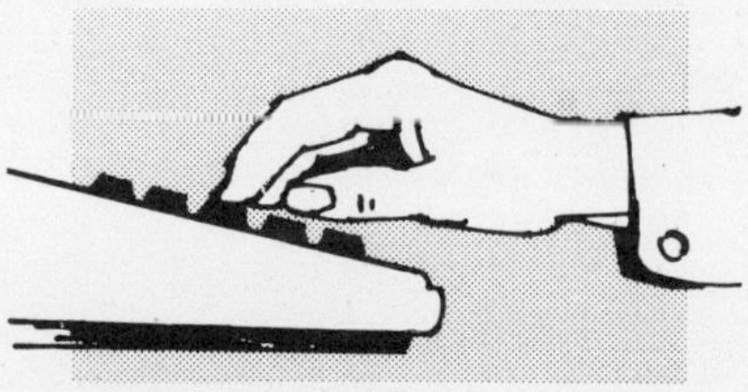

HANDS – Flat across backs; fingers **curved** (Manual); **slightly** curved (Electric/Electronic)
WRISTS – Level; **not** supported by machine
FINGER-TIPS – Resting **on** Home Keys (Manual); **slightly** above, **when power on,** (Electric/Electronic)
THUMBS – Half an inch above space bar (right); close to first finger (left)

Curve of hand - Electric/Electronic

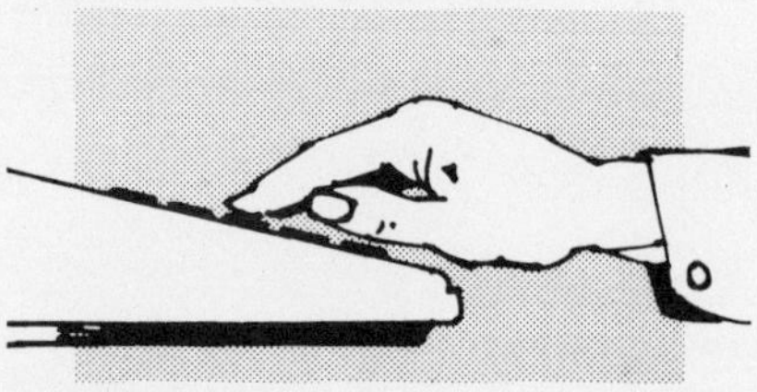

HEAD – Erect; turned towards book
ELBOWS – Close to body but relaxed
ARMS – With arms **loose**, but **almost motionless**, BEGIN TO TYPE, remembering that the following techniques are **essential** to good touch-typing:

1. THE STRIKING OF KEYS MUST BE SHARP – **MANUAL MACHINES**
   A **LIGHTER** TOUCH IS REQUIRED FOR OPERATION OF **ELECTRIC & ELECTRONIC MACHINES**
2. EYES MUST BE ON THE BOOK/COPY AT **ALL** TIMES
3. THE CARRIAGE MUST BE RETURNED **FIRMLY** AND **FULLY,** AND THE CARRIER **GENTLY,** WITHOUT LOOKING UP
4. THE SPACE BAR MUST BE **EVENLY** AND **GENTLY** OPERATED

PARTS OF THE TYPEWRITER

Figure 1

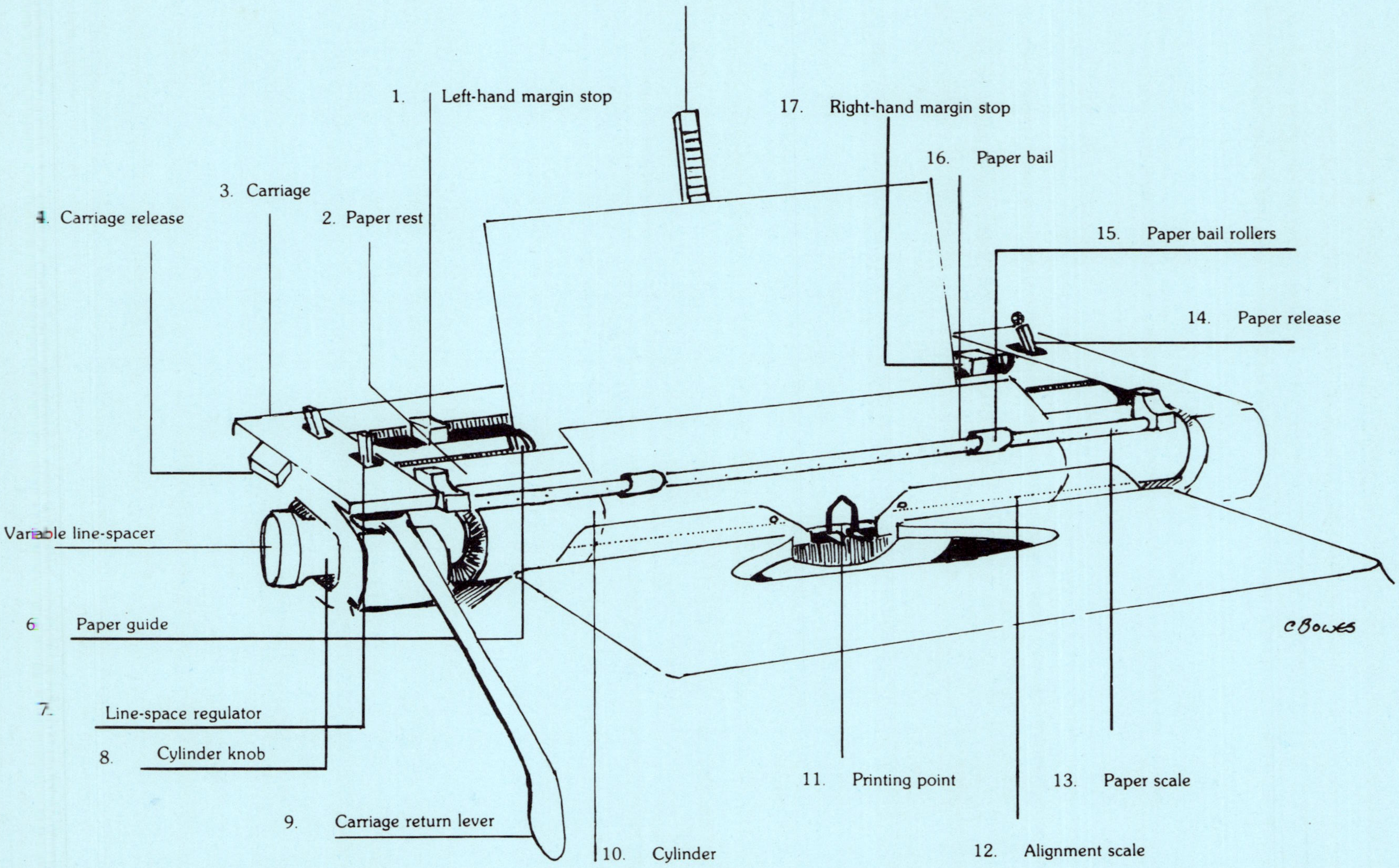

ELECTRONIC MACHINE VARIATIONS:

1 and 17 Replaced by special keys on keyboard.
3 Replaced by the carrier (moving part housing the typewheel, cassette ribbon, etc.).
4 The space bar moves the carrier to the right and the back-space key takes it to the left.
9 Replaced by return key (on keyboard).
12 Sometimes placed near printing point (11) or omitted when the machine has automatic paper insertion.
13 Sometimes placed on the panel above the keyboard.

LESSON 1

PREPARATION

1. Place the book to the right of your typewriter.
2. Have ready on the left, two sheets of A4 (210 x 297 mm) typing paper and a ruler.

PARTS OF THE TYPEWRITER

1. Study the diagram (Parts of the Typewriter - Figure 1) and compare it with your machine.
2. Check the typewriter manufacturer's handbook to assess whether your machine has Elite or Pica type; alternatively measure with a ruler a 1 inch (25mm) section of the PAPER SCALE(13). If your typewriter has Elite type (12 pitch), the PAPER SCALE will show 12 character spaces (marks on the scale) to 1 inch (25 mm); if Pica type (10 pitch) it will show 10 character spaces to 1 inch (25 mm).

SETTING MARGINS AND LINE-SPACE REGULATOR

1. Set the left MARGIN STOP(1) at 20 (Elite) or 12 (Pica).
2. Place the right-hand MARGIN STOP(17) at the extreme right of the CARRIAGE(3). (Where margins are set by a lever/key, set the **left-hand** margin only.)
3. Set the LINE-SPACE REGULATOR(7) on position number one (single-line spacing). Single-line spacing means that **no** space will be left between the lines of type.

INSERTING PAPER

1. Check that the PAPER GUIDE(6) is in line with '0' on the PAPER SCALE.
2. Raise the PAPER BAIL(16).
3. With your left hand, insert two sheets ot A4 size paper (one acting as a backing sheet) into the machine against the PAPER GUIDE. As you feed in from the back with your left hand, turn the right-hand CYLINDER KNOB (opposite 8) away from you with your right hand, until the paper is level with the top of the CYLINDER(10).
4. Straighten the paper, if necessary, by pulling the PAPER RELEASE LEVER(14) forward, adjusting the paper and pushing the PAPER RELEASE LEVER back into position.
5. Lower the PAPER BAIL making sure that the ROLLERS(15) are spaced to divide the paper into three.
6. Repeat the above drill (2-5) several times, pulling the PAPER RELEASE LEVER forward before taking the paper from the machine and pushing it back into position after extracting the paper. NEVER PULL PAPER OUT OF THE MACHINE WITHOUT FIRST PULLING THE PAPER RELEASE LEVER FORWARD!

   N.B. Some Electronic machines have an automatic paper insertion facility.

APPENDIX

Backward Feed. If an addition or correction has to be made to a typed document of several pages, already stapled together, it can be done **without** removing the staple by inserting a sheet of paper into the machine in the normal way, inserting the **bottom** of the page to be corrected between the cylinder and the sheet of paper and turning the cylinder **towards** you until the page (after adjustment) is in the correct position for the correction/addition.

Footnotes. A footnote should be typed at the bottom of the page on which the reference occurs – before the 1 inch (25 mm) margin – in single-line spacing. A line is typed from margin to margin, two spaces down from the text and the footnote(s) typed two spaces from the line. The reference marks, asterisk, dagger, double dagger (used in that order), are typed immediately after the word in the text, but one space should be left between the symbol and the first word in the footnote. **Footnotes in work for the printer** must be inserted immediately after the line containing the reference, in double-line spacing, with a typed line above and below. (See also Lesson 24 – Combination Characters.)

Half-space Corrections. To avoid re-typing because of the omission of one letter from a word, it is possible to insert an additional letter **after** erasing the incorrect word. To replace 'an' with 'and', for instance, move the printing point in line with the last letter of the previous word, and: a) on a manual - tap the space bar once, press the space bar and **hold it down,** type 'a', release and hold it down again, type 'n', release and hold it down, type 'd'. b) on an electric or electronic - press the '½-space' key, then type 'and'. (A three-letter word will now be in a space for four letters, with a half-space on either side.)

Justifying. To justify (make even) a right-hand margin (for Poetry 'hook in', Contents, etc.) it is necessary to deduct the number of characters in the word(s) to be typed, from the right-hand margin (or back-space the number of characters from the margin stop) before typing the word(s) at the calculated point on the scale.

Stencils (Manual Machines). Before typing a stencil, make sure that the type is clean and that the ribbon-adjuster is on the disengaged ('white') position. A sheet of carbon paper (sometimes already attached) should be inserted between the backing sheet and the stencil, **coated side up,** so that the work can be read before removing it from the machine. (Errors should be corrected with **stencil** correcting fluid.) Punctuation marks and open letters such as 'o' and 'e' should be typed with a lighter touch and a heavier pressure put on 'm' and 'w'. Any lines, accents or other additions should be made with a stylus pen over a hard board.

RETURNING THE CARRIAGE/CARRIER

1. Grip firmly CYLINDER KNOBS(8) placed either side of the CARRIAGE(3). Without moving your hands, push down the CARRIAGE RELEASE LEVERS(4) with **first** fingers and move the CARRIAGE to the extreme left. Release. (On **electronic machines,** hold down the space bar to bring the CARRIER to the right-hand margin.)
2. With your left hand, grip the CARRIAGE RETURN LEVER (9) firmly between the first finger and thumb - the joint at the base of the finger fitting into the groove in the lever. Check that the palm is facing downwards so that your hand will travel easily across the machine, before giving the CARRIAGE RETURN LEVER a firm push to return the CARRIAGE to the left MARGIN STOP. (On **electric/electronic machines,** the carriage return lever is replaced by a carriage return KEY placed on the right of the keyboard. This is operated by the little finger on the right hand.)
3. Follow the routine (1-2) several times.

As you will see, the CARRIAGE/CARRIER RETURN LEVER/KEY not only returns the CARRIAGE/CARRIER, but also moves the paper up one line space.

THE HOME KEYS

4	3	2	1	1	2	3	4

Left-hand Fingers **Right-hand Fingers**

THE HOME KEYS

1. Place your finger-tips on the HOME KEYS – so called because they are the keys on which the fingers 'live'.
2. Keeping your right hand in position, lift your left hand to the CARRIAGE RETURN LEVER and back to the HOME KEYS, until you can return to the HOME KEYS without looking at the keyboard.
3. **If your machine is electric or electronic,** practise reaching with the right-hand little finger from semi-colon to RETURN KEY and back to semi-colon, keeping your fingers **slightly above** the HOME KEYS. (Power off for all 'finger movement' practice.)

FINGER MOVEMENTS

1. Read carefully 'BEFORE YOU TYPE CHECK. . .' (Page V), as to become an even, accurate touch-typist you will need to refer regularly to the 'Check' list to ensure that you are carrying out the correct routine before beginning to type.

An index (a **detailed** alphabetical list of content) may be typed in one column at the centre of an A4 page, or in 2 columns when the items to be included are narrow (as example). Single-line spacing is normally used, leaving double between each letter of the alphabet.

Exercises:

1. Type a copy of the contents, adding the heading 'Contents' in spaced capitals at the centre or blocked at the left margin.
2. Type a copy of the extract from an index, adding the heading in spaced capitals either at the centre or blocked at the left margin.
3. Copy contents and indexes from books in your possession.
4. Type a contents and/or index for your book, booklet, essay, thesis, report, etc.

Figure 2

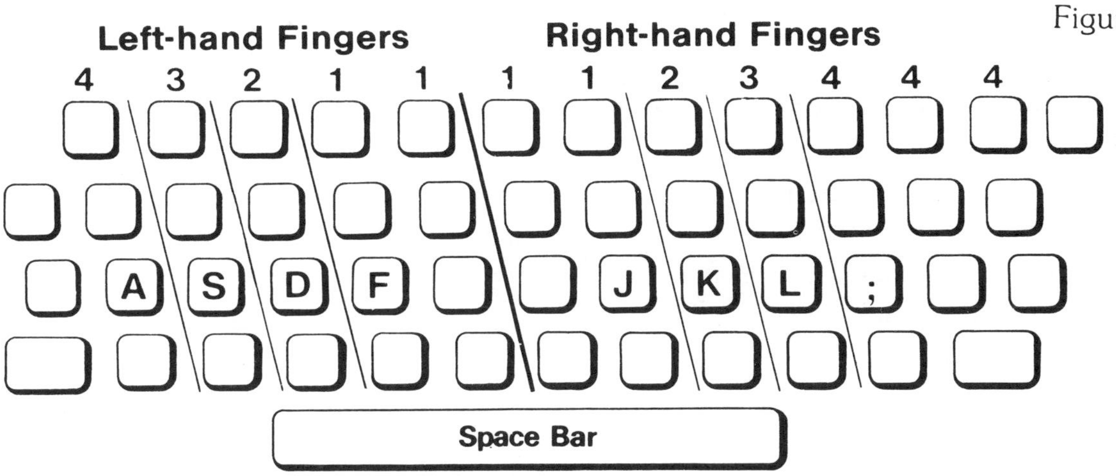

2. Place your finger-tips on the HOME KEYS, and **without typing,** practise finger movements. Beginning with the little finger (4th) on the left hand, bounce from key to key without striking, saying the names of the letters (a s d f) to yourself, or out loud, until you know where the keys are placed and can **feel** that your hand is in the correct position without looking down at the keyboard.
3. Carry out the same drill beginning with the 4th finger on the right hand (; l k j). IF YOUR WRISTS AND ELBOWS ARE NOT LEVEL YOU WILL FIND MOVEMENTS DIFFICULT; ADJUST YOUR CHAIR OR USE A CUSHION TO ACHIEVE THE CORRECT POSITION.

THE SPACE BAR

1. Repeat finger movements as above, but this time, between each group of four letters, tap the SPACE BAR (Figure 2) with the side of your **right** thumb. As you will see, the SPACE BAR moves the CARRIAGE/CARRIER one space. DO NOT HOLD THE BAR DOWN, BUT PRESS AND RELEASE SMOOTHLY.
2. Return the CARRIAGE/CARRIER.

STRIKING THE KEYS

1. Place your fingers on the HOME KEYS.
2. Check your hand positions and that fingers are curved and then strike sharply with finger-tips, the keys in **Exercise I**, saying aloud "a s d f space - ; l k j space", etc. YOU WILL NEED TO LIFT YOUR FINGERS SLIGHTLY, BUT DO NOT MOVE FROM THE HOME KEYS.

Exercise I

`asdf ;lkj asdf ;lkj asdf ;lkj asdf ;lkj asdf ;lkj` (Return the Carriage/Carrier.)

3. Repeat Exercise I **three times,** listening to the rhythm of the keys as they come into contact with the paper. If you are striking them correctly, each stroke will take the same amount of time, including the operation of the space bar. You should hear "tap, tap, tap, tap, space, tap, tap, tap, tap, space" to the count of five.

REPORTS

A report of an event, meeting or interview is normally arranged in logical sequence under shoulder headings (paragraph headings may be used when only one paragraph is being written under each heading). It may be typed in single-line spacing, but if it is to be read aloud or to be sent to a printer, it should be typed in double-line spacing on one side of A4 paper – see also Typescript for the Printer. (An annual report of a club/organization should be typed in the same way and include details of membership, social events, fund raising, etc.)

Exercises:

1. Copy a report in your possession or from your local newspaper.
2. Compose and type a report of
   a) a meeting you attended on behalf of a colleague/organization, **or**
   b) a local event for submission to a newspaper, **or**
   c) an interview, conducted by you.

CONTENTS/INDEXES

Contents (a **summary** of subject-matter) should be typed with a justified right-hand margin (see Appendix) at the centre of an A4 page. Leader dots are sometimes included and may be typed either singly at 5, 10, 15, 20, etc. on the scale, or in pairs at the same points (as example).

Chapter		Page
	Introduction	ii
1	THE BIRTH	1
2	LONDON	30
3	THE LONGING	52
4	JOHN	71
5	GOODBYE TO LONDON	96
6	HOME	108

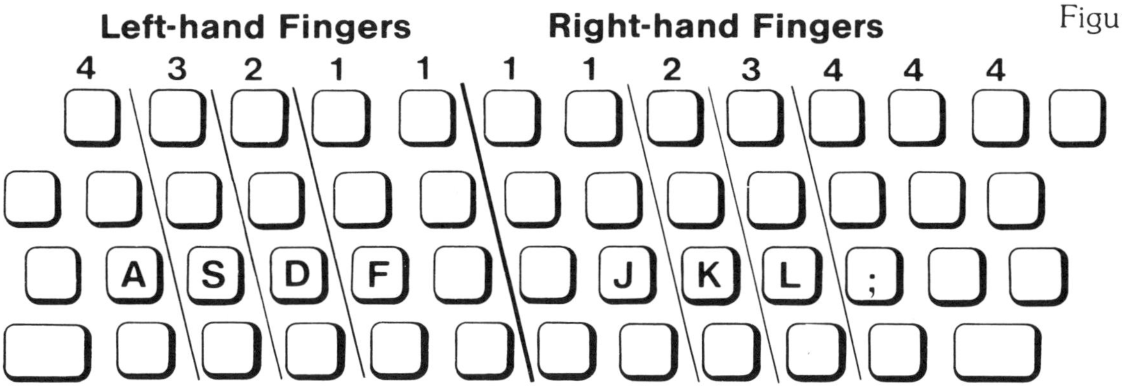

Figure 3

4. Keeping your eyes on the copy, type each of the following lines **three times,** leaving one line-space between each set of three (i.e. return the CARRIAGE/CARRIER and push the CARRIAGE RETURN LEVER/CARRIER RETURN KEY once more). **Remember to say the letters (and spaces) as you strike them.** This time the count will be "tap, tap, tap, space". (No space is left after the final group of letters in each line.)

Exercise II

```
fff jjj fff jjj fff jjj fff jjj fff jjj fff jjj fff jjj fff jjj

ddd kkk ddd kkk ddd kkk ddd kkk ddd kkk ddd kkk ddd kkk ddd kkk

sss lll sss lll sss lll sss lll sss lll sss lll sss lll sss lll

aaa ;;; aaa ;;; aaa ;;; aaa ;;; aaa ;;; aaa ;;; aaa ;;; aaa ;;;
```

CORRECTING FAULTS

1. Study your typewriting. If you have a second impression round the typed letters (shadowing) you are leaving the keys down too long. If some letters are lighter or darker than others, your touch is not yet even. **Touch is automatically adjusted on electric and electronic machines.**
2. To correct faults, type further lines of the above exercise, listening carefully to rhythm – the equal timing of each stroke – and making sure that you are releasing each key immediately after striking. Also check that all fingers, including the little fingers, are curved, **not straight,** as they strike the keys.

Note: To establish rhythm and the recommended pace for the beginner, you will find it helpful to practise tapping your fingers on a table in the order 4, 3, 2, 1, to the ticking of a clock, or watching the second hand on a watch. This exercise will also help to strengthen the little fingers.

ESSAYS

An essay should be typed in double-line spacing on one side of A4 paper, using a wide left-hand margin (1½ inches – 2 inches or 38 mm – 51 mm) and a 1 inch (25 mm) right-hand margin. Footnotes (see Appendix) should be typed at the bottom of the page on which the reference occurs. The work is normally arranged in logical sequence under shoulder headings and all pages, other than the first, numbered within the top or bottom 1 inch (25 mm) margin.

Exercises:

1. Study typed or printed essays in your college or public library.
2. Type at least three A4 pages of your own notes in the form of an essay.
3. Type a title page.

THESES

A thesis should be typed in double-line spacing on one side of A4 paper, using a wide left-hand margin (1½ inches – 2 inches or 38 mm – 51 mm) and a 1 inch (25 mm) right-hand margin. Small comparative tables may be included within the text or larger tables typed on a separate page and inserted at the appropriate place. If the table is too wide for A4 portrait paper, it may be typed on A4 landscape – in this case it would be necessary to leave the wide margin at the **top** of the sheet. Most college and university libraries contain samples of typed and printed theses and some universities issue a booklet for the use of typists which includes specific rules for the form that footnotes and bibliographic references should take.

Exercises:

1. Study typed and printed theses.
2. Type at least three A4 pages of your own notes in the form of a thesis.
3. Type a title page.

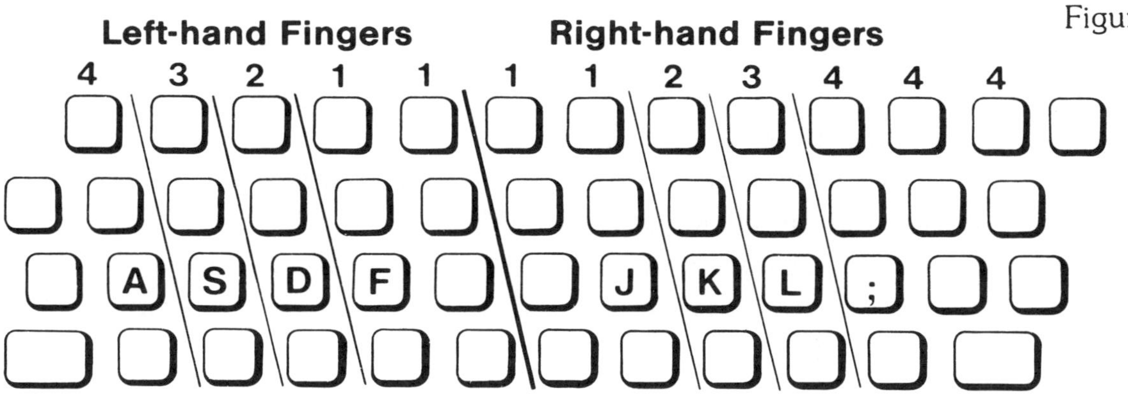

Figure 4

LESSON 2

REVISION

1. Insert 2 sheets of A4 paper (one acting as a backing sheet) into the machine.
2. Set left MARGIN STOP at 20 (Elite) or 12 (Pica).
3. Set the LINE SPACE REGULATOR on '1' (single-line spacing).
4. Refer to 'BEFORE YOU TYPE CHECK . . .'
5. Saying the names of the letters (and spaces) as you strike them, type each of the following lines **three times**, leaving one line-space between each set of three. **Remember to concentrate on rhythmic movements and, on manual machines, to bounce your fingers off the keys as you type.**

Exercise I

```
fff jjj fff jjj ddd kkk ddd kkk sss lll sss lll aaa ;;; aaa ;;;

jaj jaj jaj jaj kak kak kak kak lal lal lal lal ;a; ;a; ;a; ;a;

asa asa asa asa ada ada ada ada afa afa afa afa ala ala ala ala
```

IMPROVEMENT PRACTICE

1. Check your work to see if you have any of the **faults** outlined at the end of Lesson 1 under the heading 'Correcting Faults' and if so, type further lines of the above exercise to remedy these (manual machine users).
2. If you are still unable to return the CARRIAGE/CARRIER and return to the HOME KEYS without looking away from the copy, practise the movements given in Lesson 1 under the heading 'The Home Keys'.

The following is a sample layout for a **stage** play. All stage directions should be underscored (preferably in red) and each act typed on a new page with a 'Dropped Head' (see Novels). Scripts for **radio** are typed in the same manner, but sound effects or technical directions must be typed in **capitals** within brackets. For a **television** drama script, a wider margin must be left before the speeches begin (allowing for camera directions on the left), and each 'frame' is numbered on a line drawn from margin to margin. (Specimen pages of television and radio drama scripts can be found in "Writing for the BBC" – BBC Publications.)

MRS BLACK is standing by the kitchen table unwrapping a sliced loaf. AVRIL enters yawning; buttoning the cuffs of her blouse.

MRS BLACK Good morning darling.

AVRIL (Sitting down at the table and pouring a cup of tea)

'Morning Mum. Any mail?

MRS BLACK (Putting bread into toaster)

No, the postman hasn't been yet. Are you expecting a letter from Roger?

AVRIL Yes, he did promise he'd write before the week-end. I hope he's got leave.

MRS BLACK (Sitting down opposite Avril)

Is it getting serious between you two?

AVRIL Well . . . well, yes, I suppose it is.

MRS BLACK You know your father doesn't like him darling.

AVRIL I'm the one who's going to marry him, not Dad!

MRS BLACK (Aghast) Marry?

Exercises:

1. Type a copy of the above extract.
2. Borrow plays from your local library (for stage, radio and television) and practise typing dialogue and introductory pages.
3. Type at least 3 pages of your own manuscript, taking 2 carbon copies.

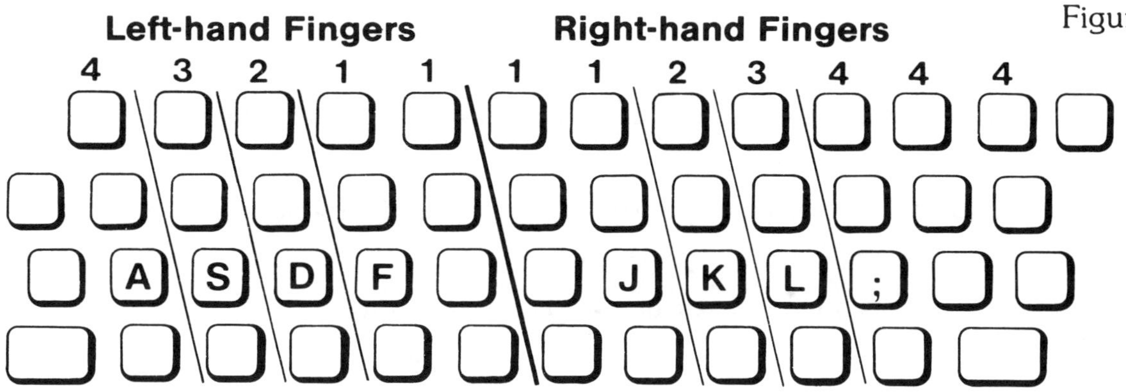

Figure 5

CONSOLIDATION

1. Following instructions and reminders outlined in paragraph 5 above, Type Exercise II.

Exercise II

```
ka ka ka ka la la la la ja ja ja ja ;a ;a ;a ;a ka la ja ;a

ad ad ad ad as as as as af af af af a; a; a; a; al al al al

dad dad sad sad fad fad lad lad dad dad sad sad fad fad lad

ask ask all all add add as; as; ask ask all all add add as;

fall fall lass lass lads lads asks asks adds adds fads fads

all ask; dad asks; ask a lad; all ask dad; a sad lass asks;

dad adds; a lad falls; a lass falls; dad asks a sad lass;
```

2. Check your work; circle all typing errors and typing faults.
3. If you have more than **four** errors (including typing faults) in any group of three lines, you will benefit from repeating the lines after taking a short break. If you have less than four errors in some groups, you have made an excellent start!

Note: Keep your typewritten exercises in a large envelope or file so that you may refer to them later in order to establish your progress.

Exercises:

1. Type a correct copy of the amended script on A4 paper in double-line spacing, using a 60-space typing line.
2. Using the printers' correction signs shown above, correct where necessary one of your own manuscripts ready for typing.
3. Type at least 3 pages from a corrected (or other) script.
4. Type a title page, indicating the approximate number of words you have typed.

DRAMA

Plays must be typed on one side of A4 paper, using margins of 1½ inches (38 mm) on the left and 1 inch (25 mm) on the right. All pages should be firmly fastened together and a protective front and back cover added, as well as introductory pages containing the following information:

Stage Play

(i) Title, author, address
(ii) Synopsis of acts and scenery
(iii) List of characters

Radio/Television Play

(i) Title, author, address
(ii) Synopsis of play (including approximate length in minutes)
(iii) Cast list (with brief notes on individual characters)
(iv) List of studio sets and film sequences (TV only)

The information included in the introductory pages should be centred vertically on the page and horizontally on the typing line. All pages, other than the introductory pages, must be numbered.

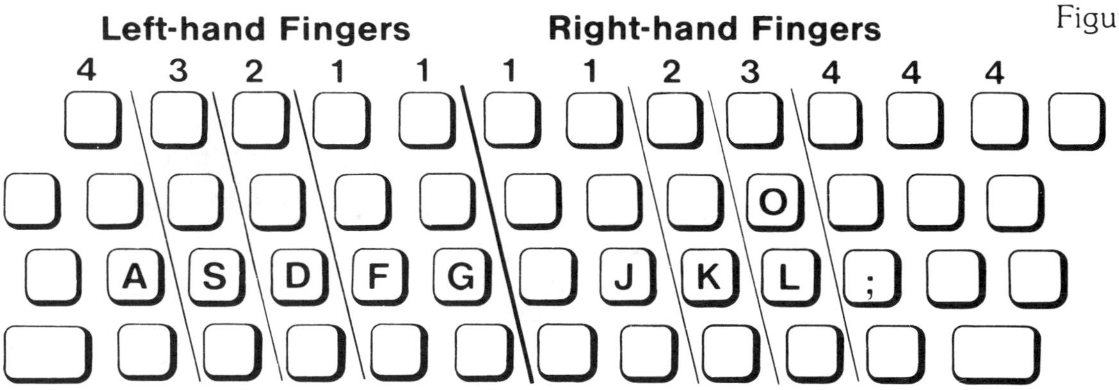

Figure 6

LESSON 3

REVISION

1. Insert A4 typing paper into the machine. **Remember to use a backing sheet in order to protect the cylinder.**
2. Set the left MARGIN STOP at 20 (Elite) or 12 (Pica).
3. Set the LINE SPACE REGULATOR on '1'.
4. Refer to 'BEFORE YOU TYPE CHECK . . .'
5. Type each of the following lines **three times,** leaving one line space between each set of three. **In order to memorize the position of the keys, remember to say each letter as you type.**

Exercise I

```
fff jjj ddd kkk sss lll aaa ;;; fff jjj ddd kkk sss lll aaa ;;;

ka ka la la ja ja ;a ;a ad ad as as af af a; a; al al ak ak as;

dad sad fad lad ask add as; lass lads adds asks falls salad all
```

6. Repeat any lines you found to be difficult.

NEW KEYS – G and O

1. Locate the keys G and O shown on the above diagram. Move finger one on the left hand from its HOME KEY F to the new key G and back to its HOME KEY, until you can move easily from home key to new key and immediately back to home key, without looking at the keyboard.
2. Practise in the same way, movements from L to O, using the third finger on the right hand.
3. Keeping your eyes on the copy, type the following line **once.**

Printers' Correction Signs. The following are the basic correction signs used by the printer. You will find them helpful to use for making amendments to your own work before the final typing. (A **complete** list of correction signs is given in "The Writers' and Artists' Year Book" – Publisher A. & C. Black.)

Marginal sign	**Sign used in text**	**Meaning**
NP or para	[or //	Make new paragraph
run on		No new paragraph required
uc or lc	— under word(s)	Type in Upper case/Lower case
word/letter/punctuation, plus caret	^	Insert letter/word/punctuation shown in margin
stet	- - - - - under word to be used	Let it stand (type original word(s)
		Close up (delete space)
#	^	Insert space
	/ through letter	Delete
trs	~	Transpose (change order of words/letters)

Example of Corrected Typescript:

uc   Applying Inside Learning to Outside Learning

When teaching typewriting governed by the rules laid down by RSA, I also teach stu dents that certain other layouts are acceptable in most job situations and that once in work, they must be guided by 'house' rules. [It is interesting to note that students soon bgein to criticise typing layouts and the untidiness of business letters and other communications they receive at home. They admit that before learning to type, most would have been quite acceptable to them.

(NP, trs, run on, stet — marginal marks)

I find this very encouraging, as I realise that the standard set is now becoming their standard and hoppefully they will continue, in a job situation to present work of a high standard ~~degree~~ of accuracy and neatness. . . .

Figure 7

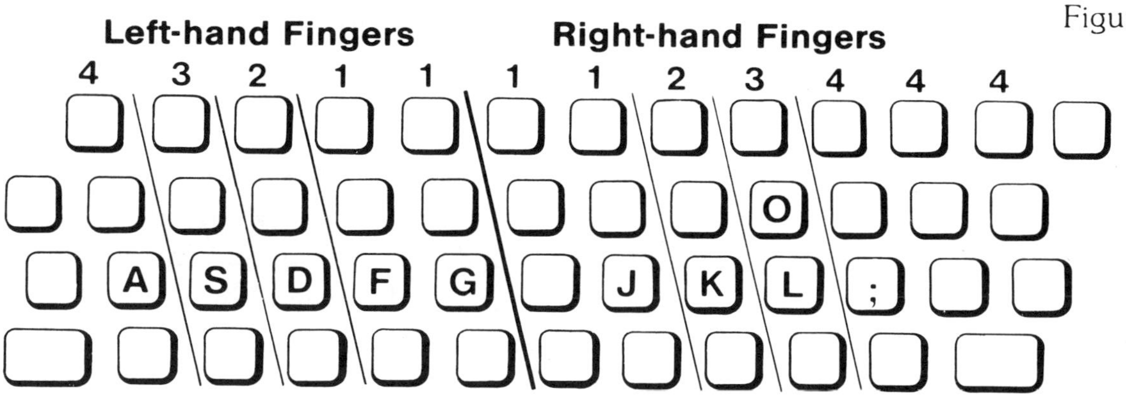

Exercise II

```
fgf fgf fgf fgf fgf fgf fgf fgf lol lol lol lol lol lol lol lol
```

4. Type Exercise II once more, concentrating this time on rhythmic movements. **Remember to say the letters and spaces as you strike them.**

5. Type each of the following lines **three times. Remember to: keep hands still; move fingers only; return to home key immediately after striking new key; leave one line space between each set of three lines.**

Exercise III

```
fff ggg fgf fgf fff ggg fgf fgf fff ggg fgf fgf fff ggg fgf fgf

fag fag jag jag sag sag lag lag fag fag jag jag sag sag lag lag

gas; gas; sag; sag; lag; lag; jag; jag; flag flag glad glad as;

gag gag lags lags sags sags fags fags flags flags glass; glass;

lll ooo lol lol lll ooo lol lol lll ooo lol lol lll ooo lol lol

so; so; go; go; do; do; of; of; so; so; go; go; do; do; of; of;

log log fog fog jog jog sog sog log log fog fog jog jog sog sog

goal goal foal foal doll doll dogs dogs loads loads sold; sold;
```

6. Take a short break before continuing.

Note: 1) If your wrists and fingers are stiff, relax them now by letting your arms hang loosely beside your body for a few minutes. 2) Check before you type once more that you are in fact holding your hands in the correct typing position (see 'Before You Type Check . . .')

TYPESCRIPT FOR THE PUBLISHER/PRINTER

Scripts submitted to a publisher must be typed in double-line spacing on one side of A4 paper, using indented paragraphs. One inch top and bottom margins should be left and a wide left-hand margin (1½ inches – 2 inches or 38 mm – 51 mm). The first page is not numbered, but should include the heading, centred on the typing line, on the 7th line from the top. All other pages should be numbered in arabic figures at the centre of the 4th line from the top (or bottom, if preferred). Printers **prefer** manuscripts to be typed to a width of 60 characters to a line as this helps them to calculate more easily the space the work will occupy – it makes your calculations easier also. (A 60-space typing line is equal to 12 words – an average word taking up 5 character spaces – and an A4 page typed in double-line spacing, leaving the correct top and bottom margins, holds 29 lines of type. This means that a full A4 page contains approximately 350 words.) Suitable margins for a 60-space line are 24 and 84 (Elite), 15 and 75 (Pica).

Articles, Short Stories and Novels should be typed as outlined above, but in the case of the novel, each chapter must begin on a fresh sheet and the headings typed as a 'Dropped Head' (i.e. the chapter number typed at the centre of the typing line, 2 – 3 inches (51 mm – 76 mm) from the top of the sheet, followed by the chapter heading, typed in capitals on the 3rd single line space below). The introduction or preface should be numbered in small roman numerals. (See also Footnotes – Appendix.)

A Title Page must be attached to all typescripts. The address of the author is typed at the top right-hand side of the sheet; the title and author's name or pseudonym in the centre of the page (see example below); the approximate number of words on the left near to the bottom margin and when indication as to the rights to be offered is included (e.g. F.B.S.R. offered), this should be typed on the right-hand side, opposite the number of words.

EMMA LOUISE GOES TO DANCING CLASSES

by

BRENDA BEAVER

IMPROVEMENT PRACTICE

1. Check your work and circle errors, including light/dark or shadowed letters (typing **faults**).
2. Repeat any group of three lines in which four or more errors occurred.

CONSOLIDATION

1. Following instructions and reminders outlined in paragraph 5 (New Keys) above, type the following phrases:

Exercise IV

```
a good dog; a good goal; a good lass; a good lad; a good dad;

a lad loads; a lad jogs; off dad jogs; a sad lass; good lass;

a lass sold a doll; dad asks a sad lass; a good lad jogs off;
```

2. Check your work. If you have more than two errors in any one line, repeat the line.

LESSON 4

PLACEMENT OF WORK

The correct placement of typewritten work is important. On A4 paper, a top and bottom margin of one inch (6 line-spaces) is normally used. This means that you begin to type on the 7th line from the top of the sheet. To do this accurately, on machines without automatic insertion, you should carry out the following procedure:

1. Insert A4 paper into the machine in the normal way (the top of the paper in line with the top of the cylinder).
2. Press in the VARIABLE LINE SPACER(5) (Figure 1) with the palm of your left hand and at the same time, turn the CYLINDER KNOBS towards you until the top of the paper is in line with the horizontal line on the ALIGNMENT SCALE(12) Release hands.
3. Using the CARRIAGE RETURN LEVER/CARRIAGE RETURN KEY, turn up **seven** single-line spaces.

If you have a LINE GUIDE(18) on your typewriter, press the lever beside it to bring it into the upright position and turn the CYLINDER KNOBS away from you until the top of the sheet contacts the LINE GUIDE. As you will see, the indicator (fully extended for A4 paper) tells you the number of spaces available before the bottom of the paper is reached.

An alternative way of assessing the placement of your work is to rule a heavy line across your backing sheet one inch from the top and another one inch from the bottom. You should begin to type one line **below** the top line (visible through your paper) and finish **before** the bottom line is reached.

Note: When typing future exercises you can avoid ‘falling off’ the paper by checking **before** you begin that you have enough line spaces to complete the whole exercise before the bottom one inch margin is reached.

Where one line does not rhyme – extract (d) – the 'odd' line is indented two spaces. (When the non-rhyming line is much shorter than the others it is indented **at least** 5 spaces.)

(d)

```
               At Farringford

Should all our churchmen foam in spite
At you, so careful of the right,
  Yet one lay-hearth would give you welcome
(Take it and come) to the Isle of Wight;

Where, far from noise and smoke of town,
I watch the twilight falling brown
  All round a careless-ordered garden
Close to the ridge of a noble down.

                         Alfred Tennyson
```

Where an extra long line occurs, 'hook-in' may be used to maintain balance (i.e. bring the last word(s) to the next line, to finish flush with the preceding line – as line 5 of the following extract).

(e)

```
Companions, a Tale of a Grandfather

I know not of what we ponder'd
  Or made pretty pretence to talk
As, her hand within mine, we wander'd
  Tow'rd the pool by the limetree walk,
While the dew fell in showers from the
                     passion flowers
  And the blush-rose bent on her stalk.

                    C. S. Calverley
```

Exercises:

1. Type the examples given above on separate sheets of A5 paper – use landscape or portrait, as appropriate.
2. Copy examples from poetry books or your own manuscripts.

Figure 8

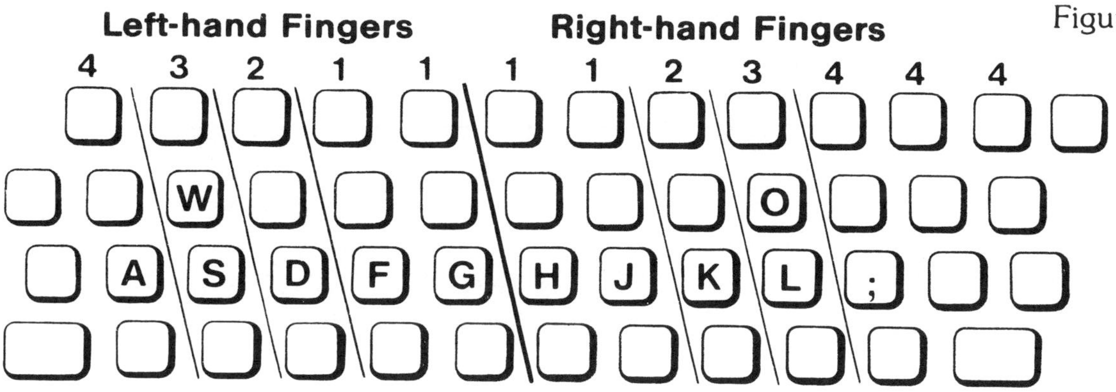

REVISION

1. Insert A4 paper. Leave a top margin of one inch (6 lines) and a left margin of 20 (Elite) or 12 (Pica).
2. Set the LINE SPACE REGULATOR on '1'.
3. Refer to 'BEFORE YOU TYPE CHECK . . .'
4. Type each of the following lines **three times,** leaving one line space between each set of three. **Remember to: keep your eyes on the copy throughout the exercise; check your work at the end of the exercise only.** (Don't be tempted to check each group of three lines!)

Exercise I

```
log fog jog sog lag fag jag sag of; go; ago off loss as; ask ass

adds fall lads asks all; logs food dogs lass gags doll good also

falls looks lags; fools soaks foals good; slogs loads fogs; goal
```

5. Repeat any lines you found to be difficult.

NEW KEYS H and W

1. Locate the keys H and W. Move the appropriate fingers (see Figure 8) from home key to new key and back to home key until the movement becomes automatic.
2. Keeping your eyes on the copy, type the following exercise **once.**

Exercise II

```
jhj jhj jhj jhj jhj jhj jhj jhj sws sws sws sws sws sws sws sws
```

3. Type the exercise once more, concentrating this time on rhythmic movements. **Remember to say the letters and spaces as you strike the keys.**

POETRY

Poems should be typed in single-line spacing with double between verses and centred on the page both horizontally and vertically. The title is normally centred over the poem and the poet's name typed at the end, flush with the right-hand margin (see Justifying – Appendix).

For blank verse and where successive lines rhyme – extracts (a) and (b) – all lines begin at the margin.

(a) John of Gaunt's Speech

This royal throne of kings, this sceptered isle,
This earth of majesty, this seat of Mars,
This other Eden, demi-paradise;
This fortress built by Nature for herself
Against infection and the hand of war;
This happy breed of men, this little world;
This precious stone set in the silver sea,
Which serves it in the office of a wall,
Or as a moat defensive to a house,
Against the envy of less happier lands;
This blessed plot, this earth, this realm, this England.

William Shakespeare

Daphne

(b)

Daphne knows, with equal ease,
How to vex and how to please,
But the folly of her sex
Makes her sole delight to vex.

Johnathan Swift

Where alternate lines rhyme – extract (c) – the second and all lines rhyming with it are indented two spaces from the margin.

'You are old, Father William'

(c)

'You are old, Father William,' the young man said,
  'And your hair has become very white;
And yet you incessantly stand on your head -
  Do you think, at your age, it is right?'

Lewis Carroll

Figure 9

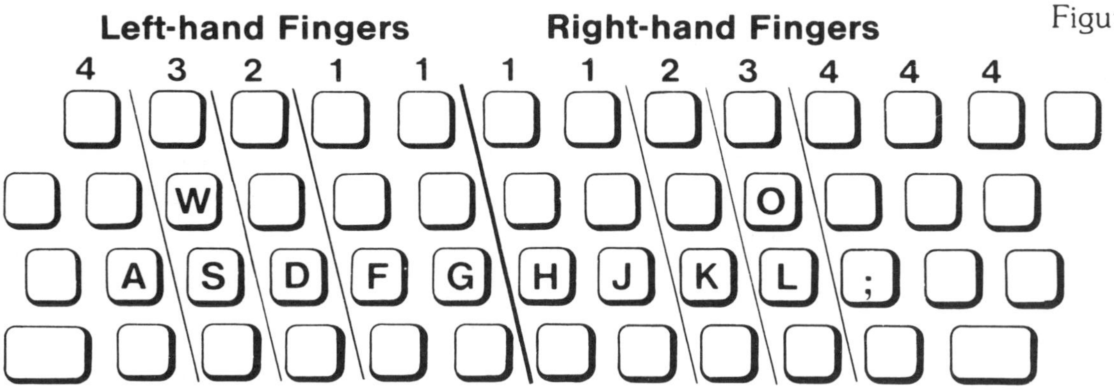

4. Type each of the following lines **three times,** listening to your rhythm and making sure that you are giving the same amount of time to the typing of each letter and space. **Remember to: return to the home key immediately after typing the new key; return the carriage/carrier promptly, keeping your eyes on the copy.**

Exercise III

```
jjj hhh jhj jhj jjj hhh jhj jhj jjj hhh jhj jhj jjj hhh jhj jhj

hag hag hog hog has has had had hag hag hog hog has has had had

sash sash hash hash dash dash lash lash gash; gash; shall shall

sss www sws sws sss www sws sws sss www sws sws sss www sws sws

was was saw saw sow sow who who was was saw saw sow sow who who

swag swag show show saws saws laws laws wash wash slows; slows;
```

IMPROVEMENT PRACTICE

If a specific word caused you to hesitate, carry out the following drill:

1. Locate the keys it contains and practise finger movements **without** typing, until you move from key to key with ease.
2. With eyes on the copy, type a complete line of the difficult word.
3. Repeat the line in which the word occurred.

CONSOLIDATION

1. Following instructions and reminders given in paragraph 4 ('New Keys') above, type the following exercise.

Exercise IV

```
odd ago fog lad off has jog was sow law how all so; saw as; jag

also look gosh slow sags goal swag fool soak good dash hood ask

shoal flash shall glass salad dolls halls shawls flasks shoals;
```


continued over

RULED TABLES

When typing ruled (boxed) tables, the horizontal lines should be inserted by using the underscore on the typewriter and the vertical lines in black ink, after removing the work from the machine. In the table shown below, 3 spaces have been left between the columns and 2 spaces on either side of the table, but when a narrow table is to be displayed on a large sheet, more space may be left between columns to make the work look balanced. (When 5 spaces are left between columns, 3 spaces should be left on either side of the table and when 7 spaces are left between columns, 4 spaces should be left on either side.)

COMPARISON OF SALES FIGURES IN £ STERLING

Appliances	March	April	May
Cookers	45,781	41,057	50,802
Dishwashers	21,070	25,100	27,350
Refrigerators	27,860	30,050	36,872
Freezers	59,534	70,304	83,430
Water Heaters	60,005	57,203	59,832
Fires	35,022	32,469	29,050
Central Heating	288,751	250,750	205,495

Exercises:

1. Type a copy of the table on A5 portrait paper, typing the horizontal lines **one** space before and after the column headings and **one** space below the last line – use the margin release to extend the lines 2 character spaces on either side of the table. BEFORE REMOVING FROM THE MACHINE, make pencil marks on the top and bottom lines, 2 spaces back from the tab points set for each column, to indicate the point at which vertical lines should be drawn.
2. Using a black pen, draw in the vertical lines and erase pencil marks.
3. Type the table on A5 landscape paper, leaving 5 spaces between columns.

Figure 10

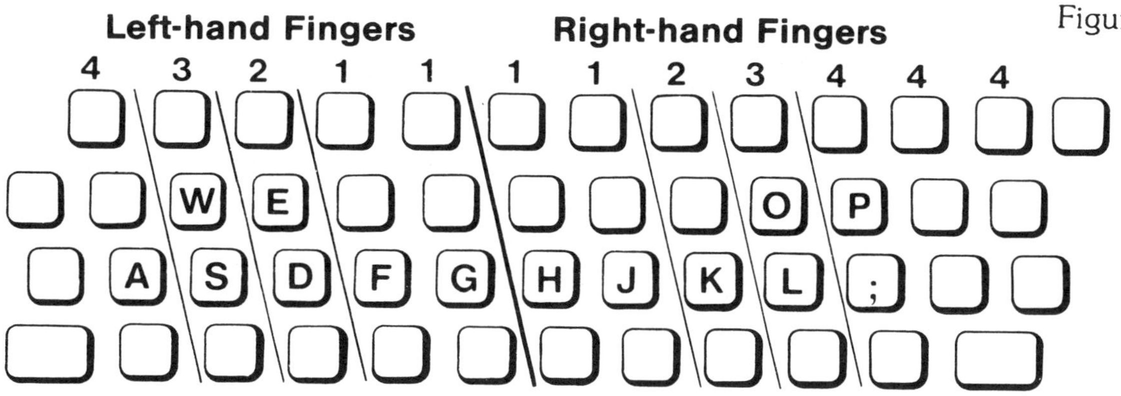


```
look dad; a hag had a shawl; a lass has a salad; a good lad;

do go dad; a lass was good; a slow lad; a lass has a hood;

dad has a hog; a lad has swag; ask dad; a good goal; a fool;
```

2. Check your work. (If you have incorrect spacing between words, you are omitting to say "space" between them.)
3. If you have more than two errors in any line, carry out improvement practice as outlined above.

LESSON 5

REVISION

1. Insert A4 paper into the machine. **Remember to leave a one inch (25 mm) top margin.**
2. Set the left MARGIN STOP at 20 or 12.
3. Set the LINE SPACE REGULATOR on '1'.
4. Refer to 'BEFORE YOU TYPE CHECK . . . '
5. Type each of the following lines **three times,** leaving one line space between each set of three. **Remember to: say each letter and space as you strike the keys; keep your eyes on the copy from beginning to end of the exercise.** PAY SPECIAL ATTENTION TO THE TYPING OF DOUBLE LETTERS – IT IS IMPORTANT THAT YOU GIVE THE SAME AMOUNT OF TIME TO EACH STROKE.

Exercise I

```
hog hag fog fag log lag jog jag off of; so; do; lad fad gad dad

ask was has how dad owl low sow saw as; ass sad sag go; dog had

loss lass fall wall laws saws adds sags show wool asks adds wow
```

6. Repeat any lines you found to be difficult.

NEW KEYS E and P

1. Locate the keys E and P. Move the appropriate fingers from HOME KEY to NEW KEY and back to HOME KEY until the movement becomes automatic.

MENUS

Menus should be centred vertically on the page and each line centred horizontally. Courses are normally typed in single-line spacing, leaving treble spacing between (i.e turn up 4). In the following example, spaced asterisks have been used as a decorative division between the courses.

T H E   T O L L G A T E   H O T E L

Dinner and Dance (£8 inclusive)

MENU

French Onion Soup
Fruit Juice
Prawn Cocktail
Duck Pâté

* * *

Grilled Chicken with Mushroom Sauce
Baked Trout with Almonds
Escalope of Veal Cordon Bleu
Entrecôte Steak Chasseur

All above dishes served with
Sauté Potatoes and a
Selection of Fresh Vegetables

* * *

Sweet Trolley
Cheese Board

* * *

Coffee and Mints

* * *

Exercises:

1. Type a copy of the menu on A5 (portrait) paper, inserting accents in ink.
2. Compose a menu, but this time make a decorative border ½ inch (13 mm) from the edge of the paper, using one of the combinations of characters shown below. (Type top and bottom borders first and then insert the paper lengthwise to type the side borders.)

o-o-o-o-o-o   /-/-/-/-/-/   @@@@@@@@   %%%%%%%%   * * * * * * * * *

Figure 11

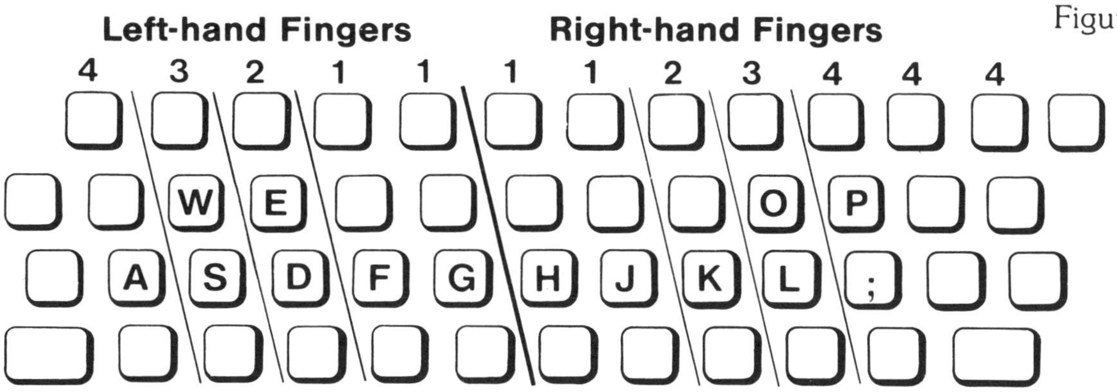

2. Keeping your eyes on the copy, type the following exercise **once.**

Exercise II

```
ded ded ded ded ded ded ded ded ;p; ;p; ;p; ;p; ;p; ;p; ;p; ;p;
```

3. Type the exercise once more, concentrating this time on rhythmic movements.
4. Following instructions and reminders given in paragraph 5 (Revision), type the following exercise. **Return to home key immediately after striking new key.**

Exercise III

```
ddd eee ded ded ddd eee ded ded ddd eee ded ded ddd eee ded ded

sea sea see see lea lea lee lee sea sea see see lea lea lee lee

he; he; she she we; we; feed feed lead lead weed weed head head

keel heed seek lake seed dead goes foes leaks deeds sells sews;

;;; ppp ;p; ;p; ;;; ppp ;p; ;p; ;;; ppp ;p; ;p; ;;; ppp ;p; ;p;

pop pcp pad pad peg peg pea pea pop pop pad pad peg peg pea pea

gap gap lap lap pa; pa; dope dope hope hope soap soap flop flop

peas pass pose keep peep jeep peal pool weeps peals seeps leaps
```

5. Check your work. If some words caused difficulty, carry out improvement practice as outlined in Lesson 4.

CONSOLIDATION

1. Following instructions and reminders given in paragraph 5 (Revision) type the following exercise.

Exercise IV

```
page pages poke poked please pleased hope hopes shape shaped he

jeeps sheep shop shoal shell shall we wee weep wall weeds shade

swell sleep slaps slope sloped slow slowed flop flap flag flog;

pass passed passes was wasp pleases poses possessed shoes shops
```

continued over

(c) TRUE/FALSE

Name .... Form ...... Date ....

INSTRUCTIONS: Place a tick (✓) in the correct box. (One mark per question.) Time allowed - 15 minutes.

1. A5 paper is suitable for a letter containing a maximum of 400 words.

TRUE	
FALSE	

2. Display paragraphs or columns to be typed within a fully-blocked letter should begin at the margin.

TRUE	
FALSE	

Exercises:

1. Type a copy of the MULTIPLE CHOICE test paper.
2. Type a copy of the COMPLETION test paper, leaving equal space for answers.
3. Type a copy of the TRUE/FALSE test paper. When making the boxes, use the underscore for horizontal lines (half a space above and below TRUE/FALSE) and draw in the vertical lines after taking the paper from the machine.
4. Compose and type a full-length test paper related to your subject.

Note: If test papers are to be photocopied, vertical lines, ticks, etc. should be drawn in with a **black** pen. When typed on a stencil ready for duplication (see Appendix) lines and other additions should be drawn with a stylus.

Figure 12

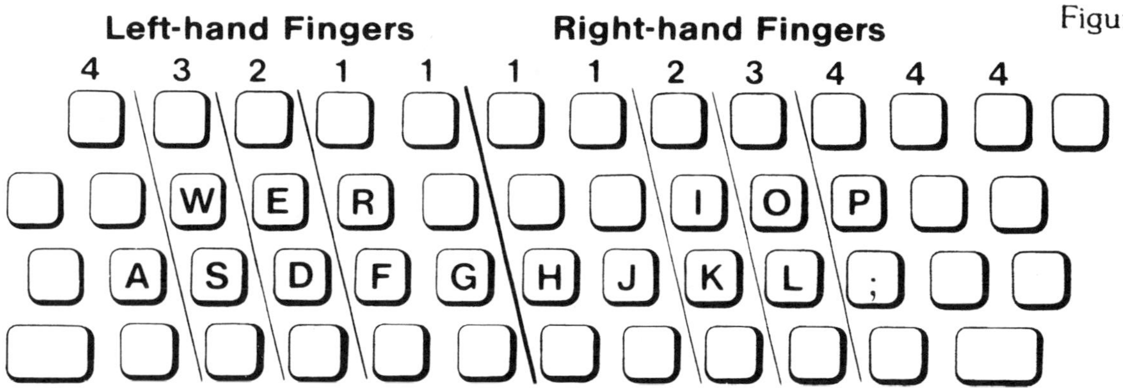


```
how she sleeps; she had a pad; she was slow; a page was passed;

we shall pass a shop; we do hope she was good; she was so slow;

please pass a salad; dad was asleep; he saw a page; he was well
```

2. Check your work. If you have more than two errors in any line, carry out improvement practice (Lesson 4).

LESSON 6

REVISION

1. Insert paper into the machine. Set the left MARGIN STOP at 20 or 12 and the LINE SPACE REGULATOR on '1'.
2. Prepare to type.
3. Type each of the following lines **three times,** leaving one line space between each set of three. **Remember to: say the letters as you strike the keys; keep your eyes on the copy throughout the exercise; move fingers, not hands, when you reach for keys.**

Exercise I

```
sea see she we; how he; pea pop pod was saw go; had who hole

keel heed leak seed dead goes sews deed foes jeep pads lads;

please pass a flask; he passed a dog; a good goal; how slow;

she was asleep; we had pea pods; she has a salad; please go;

dad passed a slow dog; he has a good poodle; she saw a wasp;
```

4. Repeat any lines you found to be difficult.

NEW KEYS R and I

1. Locate the keys R and I and practise finger movements as in previous lessons.
2. Keeping your eyes on the copy, type the following exercise **once.**

TEST PAPERS

The following are examples of layouts for Multiple Choice, Completion and True/False test papers.

(a) MULTIPLE CHOICE

Name .... Form ...... Date ....

INSTRUCTIONS: Place a tick (✓) beside the correct answer. (One mark per question.) Time allowed - 20 minutes.

1. A semi-blocked letter, unlike a fully-blocked letter, should always include

    (a) today's date

    (b) open punctuation

    (c) an attention line

    (d) indented paragraphs

    (e) standard punctuation

2. The printers' correction sign // means

    (a) Leave 2 character spaces

    (b) Insert word/words

    (c) New paragraph

    (d) Leave 2 line spaces

    (e) Run on

(b) COMPLETION

Name .... Form ...... Date ....

INSTRUCTIONS: Complete the following by adding one word. (One mark per question.) Time allowed - 30 minutes.

1. When typing a memorandum form the number of character spaces to be left after the heading 'From' should be .... character spaces.

2. Continuation sheet details should begin on line ....

3. When typing an address on an envelope, the .... should be typed in capitals.

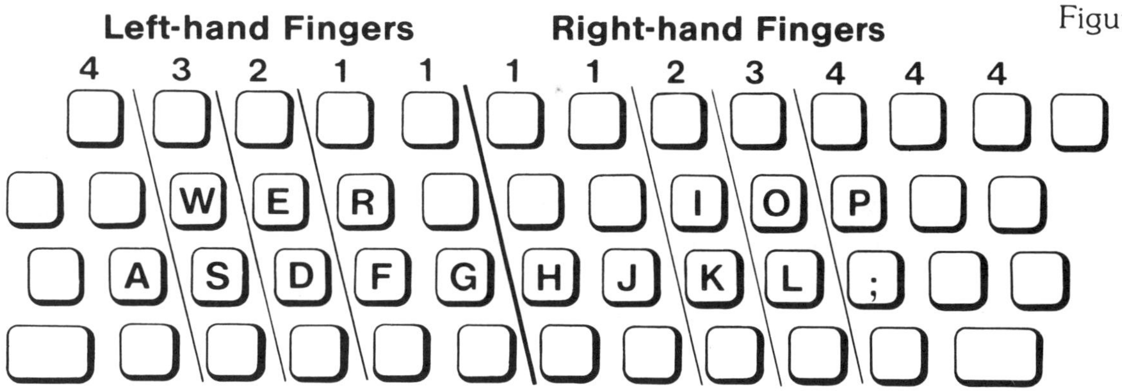

Figure 13

Exercise II

frf frf frf frf frf frf frf frf kik kik kik kik kik kik kik kik

3. Type the exercise once more, concentrating on rhythmic movements.
4. Following instructions and reminders given in paragraph 3 (Revision) type the following exercise.

Exercise III

fff rrr frf frf fff rrr frf frf fff rrr frf frf fff rrr frf frf

far far jar jar for for par par far far jar jar for for par par

row row raw raw rag rag red red rod rod are are war war her her

rage rope rare reap rear rose roll poor park hark ark; larks re

kkk iii kik kik kkk iii kik kik kkk iii kik kik kkk iii kik kik

kid kid rig rig dig dig fir fir kid kid rig rig dig dig fir fir

lid lid lip lip jig jig sip sip did did kill kill fill fill ill

hail sail fail pail rail wise lies dial girl; hairs pairs liked

5. Check your work. If some words caused difficulty, carry out improvement practice (Lesson 4).

CONSOLIDATION

1. Following instructions and reminders given in paragraph 3 (Revision) type the following exercise.

Exercise IV

hire fire sail sale pail pale here hear fear rear park lark ark;

her he; she; we; had was like liked pale paler wear wearer large

ask her here; a rare girl; she had a pearl hair slide; she asks;

how old is she; his dog is rare; his hair is fair; we like hers;

dad is here; she hopes her sail is good; we are a pair; his girl

2. Check your work. If you have more than two errors in any line, carry out improvement practice (Lesson 4).

QUESTIONNAIRES

When composing or typing a questionnaire consideration must be given to the amount of space required for the answers (e.g. much more space is necessary for an address than for a name).

JOB SEARCH

Name .... Age ...... Date ....

Which magazines did you consult? ....

....

....

Which newspapers? ....

....

....

Which newspaper or magazine contained the most advertisements in your

field? .... Date of issue ....

State the job title for which you will apply ....

Salary offered .... Name of advertiser ....

Address ....

....

Which of the following skills are included in the job description?

(Please tick.)

SHORTHAND TYPEWRITING AUDIO-TYPING BOOK-KEEPING WORD-PROCESSING

Why did you make this your first choice? ....

....

....

Exercises:

1. Type the above questionnaire in double-line spacing with 1 inch (25 mm) margins.
2. Compose and type a questionnaire related to your work/hobby.

LESSON 7

REVISION (Lessons 3–6)

If you follow carefully the revision procedure set out below you will find at the end of this lesson that you will not only have gained confidence but also developed your powers of concentration and co-ordination. This will inevitably lead to an improvement in both accuracy and speed.

1. Read thoroughly 'BEFORE YOU TYPE CHECK . . .'. Make sure that all points listed are now carried out **automatically.** Pay special attention to touch-typing techniques (1–4) and carry them out with precision as you type the following revision exercises.
2. Beginning with Lesson 3 – using a fresh sheet of paper for each lesson – type each of the exercises **once** only, leaving one line space between each **exercise** and checking your work at the end of the **lesson.** (Your eyes should therefore stay on the copy from beginning to end of each lesson.) Read all reminders **before** you begin to type. At the end of each lesson refer to paragraph 3 below.
3. Circle errors and compare your work with your original attempt. I am sure you will see an improvement. If you are still hesitating over letters/words, or have more than one error in a line, carry out the drill outlined in Lesson 4 (Improvement Practice). If you have any of the typing **faults** mentioned under 'Correcting Faults', Lesson 1, now is the time to correct these also.

You may find that this lesson will take longer than previous ones. Don't worry about this and don't rush corrective drills. If necessary, divide the lesson into two sessions. NEVER TYPE WHEN YOU ARE TIRED!

LESSON 8

REVISION

1. Insert paper into the machine. Set the left margin stop at 20 or 12 and the line-space regulator on '1'.
2. Prepare to type.
3. Type each of the following lines **three** times, leaving one line space between each set of three. **Remember to: say the letters as you strike the keys; keep your eyes on the copy throughout the exercise; keep your right hand in place when you lift your left hand to return the carriage.**

Exercise I

```
are we; he; her she who rose fill ill; wise here hears asked for;

park lark dark girl whirl rail; dries spire spear spread ahead re

we heard a girl skip; he was a slow dog; she has a large poodle;
```

4. Repeat any lines you found to be difficult.

Minutes of the Committee Meeting of the Southwood Youth Club held in the Club Room on Friday 1st December at 1930 hrs.

Present:

Mr. P. R. Atkins (Chairman)
Mrs. J. Parker
Miss B. Berryman
Miss J. Collier
Miss P. Hopkins (Secretary)

1.	APOLOGIES	Apologies for absence were received and accepted from Miss H. Tyson and Mr. D. Latham.
2.	MINUTES	The Minutes of the last meeting were read by the Secretary and signed by the Chairman as being a correct record of the proceedings.
3.	MATTERS ARISING	There were no matters arising from the Minutes.
4.	CORRESPONDENCE	There was no correspondence.
5.	ANNUAL SUMMER OUTING	It was agreed that the following suggestions be put to the Annual General Meeting: (a) A visit to London; to include a guided coach tour (b) A week-end on the Norfolk Broads (c) The British Grand Prix at Brands Hatch
6.	ANY OTHER BUSINESS	The Chairman reminded members that the redecoration of the Club Room was due to begin on 3rd January and that Youth Club Meetings would therefore be postponed for the first two weeks of the year.
7.	DATE OF NEXT MEETING	It was agreed that the next meeting of the Committee should be held in the Club Room on Friday 18th January, 19.. at 1930 hrs.

Chairman ______________________

Date ______________________

Exercises:

1. Type a copy of the notice and agenda on A4 paper using 1 inch (25 mm) margins.
2. Type a copy of the minutes on A4 paper using 1 inch (25 mm) margins.
3. Copy agendas and minutes that you have in your possession or compose them for a club or organization to which you belong.

Figure 14

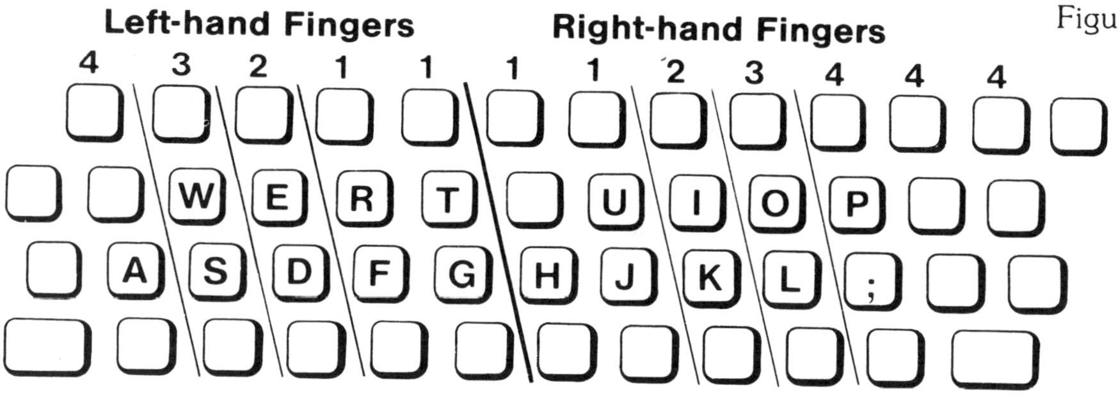

NEW KEYS T and U

1. Locate the keys T and U and practise finger movements as in previous lessons.
2. Keeping your eyes on the copy, type the following exercise **once.**

Exercise II

ftf ftf ftf ftf ftf ftf ftf ftf juj juj juj juj juj juj juj juj

3. Type the exercise once more. Concentrate on rhythmic movements.
4. Following instructions and reminders given in paragraph 3 (Revision) type the following exercise.

Exercise III

fff ttt ftf ftf fff ttt ftf ftf fff ttt ftf ftf fff ttt ftf ftf

fat fat sat sat hat hat pat pat fat fat sat sat hat hat pat pat

get get set set fit fit pit pit lot lot too too tap tap two two

to; tip tow tea tee let sat pet the that this there those these

jjj uuu juj juj jjj uuu juj juj jjj uuu juj juj jjj uuu juj juj

jug jug hug hug lug lug dug dug jug jug hug hug lug lug dug dug

due due pup pup dud dud sud sud up; up; sup sup us; us; tug tug

dull hull pull full dual flue glue suit four fudge judge sludge

5. Check your work. If necessary, carry out improvement practice (Lesson 4).

Exercises:

1. Type a copy of the C.V. (see Side Headings - pages 65/66) setting a tab stop for the date column at 82 (Elite) or 68 (Pica). Type the names and addresses of the referees in one column and use 'open' punctuation if preferred.
2. Draft and then type your own C.V. If it is longer than the example given, adopt the layout shown above when typing the names and addresses of the referees.

AGENDAS AND MINUTES

The following is an example of a notice and agenda for a committee meeting. Each member of the committee should be sent a copy of the agenda, which lists the items to be presented or discussed, seven-fourteen days before the date of the meeting.

THE SOUTHWOOD YOUTH CLUB

Chairman
P. R. Atkins

Secretary
Miss P. Hopkins

16th November, 19..

A meeting of the Committee of the Southwood Youth Club will be held in the Club Room on Friday 1st December, at 1930 hrs.

A G E N D A

1. Apologies for absence

2. Minutes of the last meeting

3. Matters arising

4. Correspondence

5. To consider suggestions for the Annual Summer Outing

6. Any other business

7. Date of the next meeting

Paula Hopkins
Hon. Secretary

As you will see from the following example of minutes, the headings must be typed in the same sequence as they appear on the agenda. Minutes (a record of the meeting) should be typed as soon as possible after the meeting and taken to the next meeting for approval of the committee and signature of the chairman.

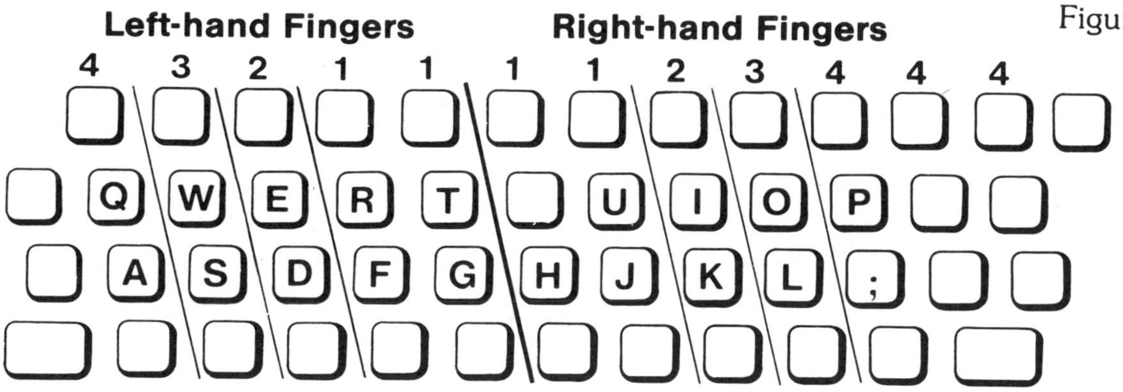

Figure 15

NEW KEY Q

1. Locate the Q key and practise finger movements.
2. Keeping your eyes on the copy, type the following exercise **once.**

Exercise IV

```
aqa aqa aqa aqa aqa aqa aqa aqa
```

3. Type the exercise once more. Concentrate on rhythmic movements.
4. Following instructions and reminders given in paragraph 3 (Revision) type the following exercise.

Exercise V

```
aaa qqq aqa aqa aaa qqq aqa aqa aaa qqq aqa aqa aaa qqq aqa aqa

quad quad quag quag quit quit quad quad quag quag quit quit qua

queue queue quart quart quite quite equal equal squat squat esq
```

5. Check your work. If necessary, carry out improvement practice.

CONSOLIDATION

1. Following instruction and reminders given in paragraph 3 (Revision) type the following exercise.

Exercise VI

```
this the; thus there their those these thou though through threw

suet duet poet quote square squash queued esquire request equate

please keep quiet; that load was squashed; he requires the suit;

how we judge those lads; their dogs are at this house; these two
```

2. Check your work. If you have more than two errors in a line carry out improvement practice.

Exercises:

1. Practise figure totalling (see Invoices – Exercise 1).
2. Type a copy of the account on A5 landscape paper. (When typing the left-hand side, set the left margin at 1 inch (25 mm) and the right margin 3 spaces from the centre of the page. Reverse the margins before typing the right-hand side – i.e. 3 spaces from the centre on the left and 1 inch (25 mm) on the right.)
3. Type a copy of the balance sheet (single-page), taking 2 carbon copies.
4. Copy any balance sheets or accounts in your possession.

CURRICULUM VITAE (C.V.)

A Curriculum Vitae should be typed on one side of A4 paper (preferably on one sheet only) using a 1" left margin.

CURRICULUM VITAE

NAME:	Julia Anne PETERSON		
ADDRESS/ TELEPHONE NUMBER:	30, The Avenue, SALISBURY, Wilts. SP5 3DB	Tel: (0722) 38753	
MARITAL STATUS:	Single		
EDUCATION:	Carisbrooke High School, Newport, I.W.		1978-81
FURTHER EDUCATION/ TRAINING:	Clerk/Typist Course - Isle of Wight College of Art & Technology, Newport, I.W.		1981-82
QUALIFICATIONS:	GCE 'O' level passes - English Language, English Literature, Geography and Maths		1981
	RSA Certificates - Office Practice Stage I, Accounting Stage II and Typewriting Stage II		1982
EXPERIENCE:	Invoice Typist/Book-keeper - J. Farmer & Sons, Timber Merchants		1982-85
	Receptionist/Typist (Relief Telephonist) - Roger Smith, Estate Agent		1985-present
HOBBIES/INTERESTS:	Reading, music, dancing and walking		
ADDITIONAL INFORMATION:	Holder of current driving licence Duke of Edinburgh (Silver) Award		 1980
REFEREES:	Mr. John Farmer, Messrs. J. Farmer & Sons, 18, Crocker Street, NEWPORT, Isle of Wight, PO30 4LT Tel: (0983) 052977	Mr. Roger Smith, 110, High Street, SALISBURY, Wilts. SP5 4LH Tel: (0722) 75028	

Figure 16

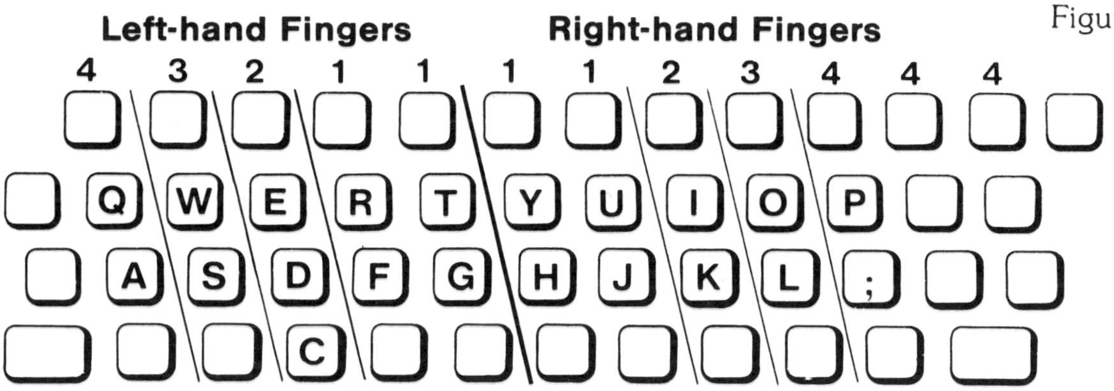

LESSON 9

REVISION

1. Insert paper into the machine. Set the left margin stop at 20 or 12 and the line-space regulator on '1'.
2. Prepare to type.
3. Type each of the following lines **three times,** leaving one line space between each set of three. **Remember to: keep your eyes on the copy; check your work at the end of the exercise only.**

Exercise I

```
he we us; she are his the this that thus those these there their;

how who to; too two what where though through throw threw thrift;

we will; she will; that will; this will; she was well; all of us;

this is; that is so; what is it; where are the lads; it was far;

go with her; tell her to look at the wasp; we are glad she is well;
```

4. Repeat any lines you found to be difficult.

NEW KEYS Y AND C

1. Locate the keys Y and C and practise finger movements as in previous lessons.
2. Keeping your eyes on the copy, type the following exercise **once.**

Exercise II

```
jyj jyj jyj jyj jyj jyj jyj jyj dcd dcd dcd dcd dcd dcd dcd dcd
```

3. Type the exercise once more. Concentrate on rhythmic movements.
4. Following instructions and reminders given in paragraph 3 (Revision) type the following exercise:

BALANCE SHEETS

Before typing a balance sheet or account, care must be taken to select the most suitably sized paper. When a large balance sheet is too wide to fit on to A4 portrait paper, the sheet may be used with the long edge at the top (landscape). For balance sheets containing several columns, it may be necessary to use A3 paper (double A4 size) folded at the centre, when used on a typewriter with a **standard** size carriage, or to join two A4 portrait sheets after typing. In either case, the longest side should be typed first and pencil marks made on the edge of the second sheet (or side) to indicate where corresponding lines and totals should be typed. (If you study the Receipts & Payments Account shown below, you will see that A5 landscape paper is suitable.)

BEAULIEU & DISTRICT SPORTS AND SOCIAL CLUB

Receipts & Payments Account for the year ended 31st December, 19..

Receipts		Payments	
	£		£
Cash in hand	10.33	Rent	80.00
Cash at bank	55.50	Heating and Lighting	55.60
Subscriptions	170.00	Stationery	26.75
Profit from		Postage	28.45
Refreshments	48.15	Cash in hand	12.22
Dances	23.05	Cash at bank	154.51
Draw	50.50		
	£357.53		£357.53

J. P. HOPKINS & SONS

Balance Sheet as at 31st March, 19..

Liabilities		Assets	
	£		£
Creditors	500.24	Leasehold premises	1,000.00
Expenses	90.00	Fixtures and fittings	350.00
Reserve Account	500.00	Stock	655.65
Capital Account	2,500.70	Debtors	746.54
		Cash in hand	30.00
		Cash at bank	808.75
	£3,590.94		£3,590.94

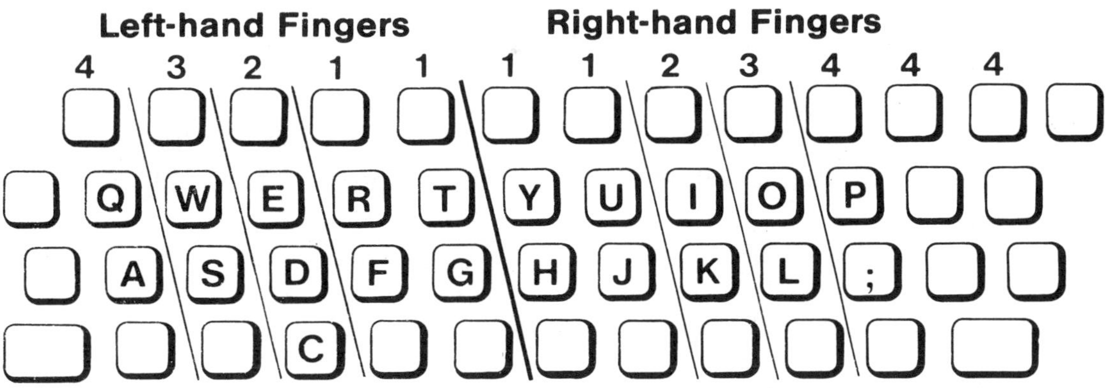

Figure 17

Exercise III

```
jjj yyy jyj jyj jjj yyy jyj jyj jjj yyy jyj jyj jjj yyy jyj jyj

jay jay hay hay gay gay say say jay jay hay hay gay gay say say

ray ray way way shy shy pay pay lay lay you you yes yes yea yea

wry try pry sky dry why day tyre they your year yell yet; youth

ddd ccc dcd dcd ddd ccc dcd dcd ddd ccc dcd dcd ddd ccc dcd dcd

cat cat cot cot car car coy coy cat cat cot cot car car coy coy

ace ace cog cog cut cut cage cage sock sock lick lick lock lock

sick sack luck copy city cite race clock flock flick grace act;
```

5. Check your work. If necessary, carry out improvement practice (Lesson 4).

CONSOLIDATION

1. Following instructions and reminders given in paragraph 3 (Revision) type the following exercise:

Exercise IV

```
patch catch which watch why; torch torches arch arches arched it

like happy estuary yearly ready partly quarterly they fetch you;

cash cashier yours years choice choose cheer cherish query queer

they are; you are; yes it is; you were there; he was there also;

the girl is happy; here is a clue; why chase her; the lucky girl

the child is here today; show her the cup; where to see the cow;
```

2. Check your work. If you have more than two errors in a line, carry out improvement practice (Lesson 4).

LESSON 10

REVISION

1. Insert paper into the machine. Set the left margin stop at 20 or 12 and the line-space regulator on single-line spacing.

2. Prepare to type.

STATEMENTS

A statement of account (a summary of a month's transactions) is normally typed on a printed document, the typist inserting the information under printed column headings, as for an invoice.

STATEMENT

OFFICE SUPPLIES LTD.
18-20, High Street,
PORTSMOUTH, Hants.
PO41 5LT

Messrs. J. Peters & Sons, — 28th February, 19..
6, The Parade,
EASTLEIGH,
Hants.
SO5 5HT — Account No. 23567

Ref.	Date		Debit	Credit	Balance
	Jan 31	Balance			4.07
330	Feb 18	Goods	18.12		22.19
869	Feb 22	Goods	216.20		238.39
C.389	Feb 24	Returns		18.12	220.27
	Feb 25	Cheque		4.07	216.20

Exercises:

1. Make 2 blank statement forms by tracing the lines from the example and marking in pencil the places where the column headings should be typed and tab stops set.
2. Type the example shown above, taking 2 carbon copies on bank paper. Take care to allow space for the larger sums of money when typing the small amounts (i.e. when typing 4.07 in the Balance column, begin 2 spaces from the tab stop set for the heading).
3. Copy a statement in your possession, or compose suitable information to complete a statement.

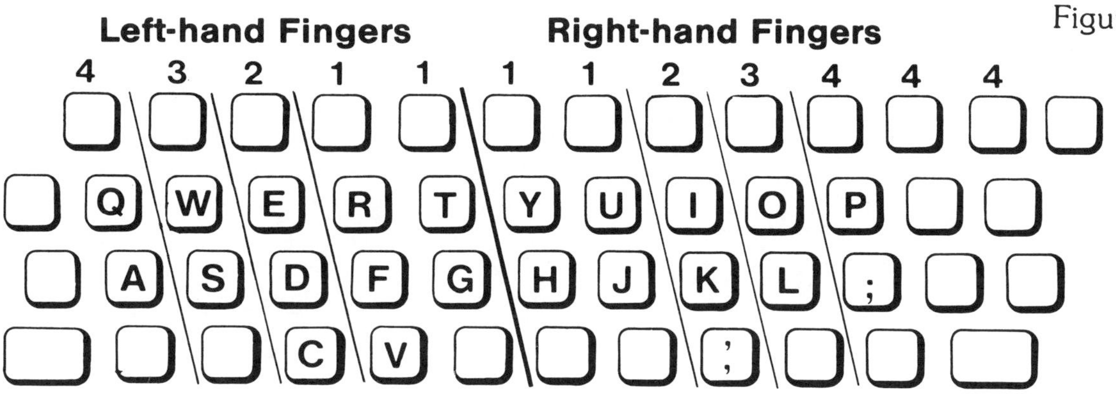

Figure 18

3. Type each of the following lines **three times,** leaving one line space between each set of three. **Remember to: keep your eyes on the copy; check your work at the end of the exercise only.**

Exercise I

```
the these this those their there they you your yours year youth;

we were where whose which what will year crust crusty cried at;

like liked list listed wish wished lurch lurched past pasted is

crashed crushed scratch scratched quest request requested tasted

yacht catch patch latch attach hatch hatchet cheer chased chose;
```

4. Repeat any lines you found to be difficult, taking care to move **fingers** only when you reach for keys.

NEW KEYS V and comma (,)

1. Locate the keys V and comma. Practise finger movements.
2. Keeping your eyes on the copy, type the following exercise **once.**

Exercise II

```
fvf fvf fvf fvf fvf fvf fvf fvf k,k k,k k,k k,k k,k k,k k,k k,k
```

3. Type the exercise once more. Concentrate on rhythmic movements and make sure that you are tucking your 'k' finger under to reach the ',' – do not move your hand/wrist position.
4. Following instructions and reminders given in paragraph 3 (Revision) type the following exercise:

THE WHITE ROSE HOTEL

Mr & Mrs Halford   Room: 18

1 August 19..

	£
One double room	36.00
Coffee	1.40
Wine	7.50
Dinner	16.80
Total (inclusive of VAT)	£61.70

Exercises:

1. Practise typing the totals of the two invoices, leaving a clear space either side of the total and making a **double** line after. (Use the interliner to move down for the **second** line.) Do not underscore the pound (£) sign.
2. Make some blank invoice forms on A4 paper by tracing the lines from the examples shown and marking in pencil the places where the headings of the columns should be typed.
3. Type the examples, taking two carbon copies of each.
4. Copy any invoices in your possession.

CREDIT NOTES

Credit notes are used for crediting goods returned or to cancel an incorrect invoice. They are usually printed and typed in red, but in other respects are typed in the same way as an invoice.

Exercise:

1. Type a credit note for items 3 and 5 on the first invoice (plus VAT).

Figure 19

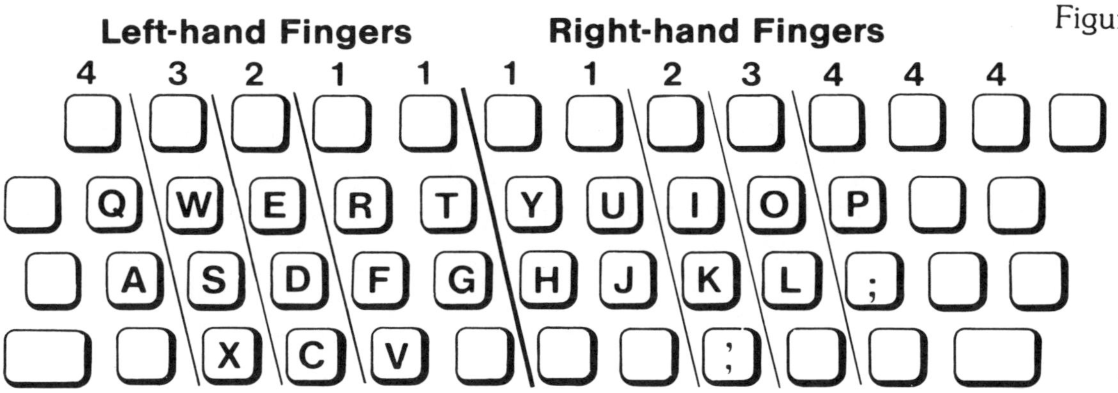

Exercise III

fff vvv fvf fvf fff vvv fvf fvf fff vvv fvf fvf fff vvv fvf fvf

vie vie via via eve eve vat vat vie vie via via eve eve vat vat

vote vote vet; vet; very very dove dove have have verse; verse;

every avoid vault visit voice vogue vocal voyage average aviary

kkk ,,, k,k k,k kkk ,,, k,k k,k kkk ,,, k,k k,k kkk ,,, k,k k,k

we, he, of, to, is, it, as, or, at, if, us, all, has, you, for;

they are, you are, here they are, it is so, yes it is, we have;

5. Check your work. If necessary, carry out improvement practice (Lesson 4).

NEW KEY X

1. Locate the X key and practise finger movements.
2. Keeping your eyes on the copy, type the following exercise **once.**

Exercise IV

sxs sxs sxs sxs sxs sxs sxs sxs

3. Type the exercise once more. Concentrate on rhythmic movements.
4. Following instructions and reminders given in paragraph 3 (Revision) type the following exercise:

Exercise V

sss xxx sxs sxs sss xxx sxs sxs sss xxx sxs sxs sss xxx sxs sxs

sex sex six six tax tax wax wax sex sex six six tax tax wax wax

lax lax vex vex cox cox axe axe exit exit axis axis text; text;

5. Check your work.

INVOICES

Firms supplying invoices for goods or services rendered, design the layout of the document according to the information they need to give. In most cases the column headings will be printed and the typist can use these as a guide when setting tab stops for the columns.

The Fireplace

Specialists in gas effect fires, surrounds, wood & multi-fuel stoves, central heating, fitted kitchens and brass & copperware etc

Mrs. J. Williams,
7, Oak Common,
Newport,
Isle of Wight.
PO36 5LT

INVOICE NO. 08382

15th September, 19..

Order No. 5687

Code	Quantity	Description	Price	Total
0991 3087	4 m	28 x 19 Pipe Lagging	0.85	3.40
0991 3086	4 m	22 x 19 " "	0.70	2.80
1212 3098	1	4 gall Tank Set		1.97
1212 3102	1	26 gall Tank Set		3.36
1352 1168	1 m	15 x 19 Foam		0.55
				12.08
		VAT @	15%	1.81
		Total	due	£13.89

9 Lower St. James Street, Newport, Isle of Wight PO30 5HE. Tel: Newport 529763
VAT No: 3391176338

CONSOLIDATION

1. Type each of the following lines **three times,** trying this time to speed up a little when typing the line for the third time.

Exercise VI

```
taxis waxes exact craft grove hover happy vexed sixty queue today

extras voices proves views; expects violets relaxed correct exit;

however gravity whatever, advertise, slippers, yesterday expected

you go to the exit, that is the correct day, they are still here;

she looks happy, take this trip today, go forward without worries
```

2. Check your work. If you have more than two errors in the **final** typing, carry out improvement practice (Lesson 4).

LESSON 11

REVISION

1. Insert paper into the machine. Set the left margin stop at 20 or 12 and the line-space regulator on single-line spacing.
2. Prepare to type.
3. Type each of the following lines **three times,** leaving one line space between each set of three. **Remember to: keep your eyes on the copy; check your work at the end of the exercise only; pay attention to rhythm.**

Exercise I

```
wax tax sax taxis sixty vexed violets several correct, youthful;

he was evil; she was good; they were happy; we are very tired;

we expect her at three; if she does arrive we will tell you;
```

4. Repeat any lines you found to be difficult, taking care to move **fingers** only when you reach for keys.

POSTCARDS

Postcards, like memos, should be typed without salutation and complimentary close. They are mainly used in acknowledgement of letters and orders or for the notification of arrival or delivery of goods. The name and address of the firm sending the postcard is normally printed on the card, together with most standard information (i.e. in the specimen card, space would be left for the date, order number and type of shoe only–the rest could be printed).

THE CASUAL SHOE SHOP
20, South Street, LONDON. SE6 2AZ

10th July, 19..

Your Order No. 261/84

We are pleased to inform you that your 'Sandra' shoes have now arrived at our store.

Will you please call to collect them within the next 14 days.

POST CARD

The Address only to be written on this side

Mrs. R. Martin,
104, Lannoy Road,
New Eltham,
LONDON.
SE9 2BL

Exercises:

1. Type a copy of the postcard shown above, using ½ inch (13 mm) margins.
2. Copy any postcards in your possession or compose some acknowledgements. (In practice, A6 paper may be used instead of postcards.)

Figure 20

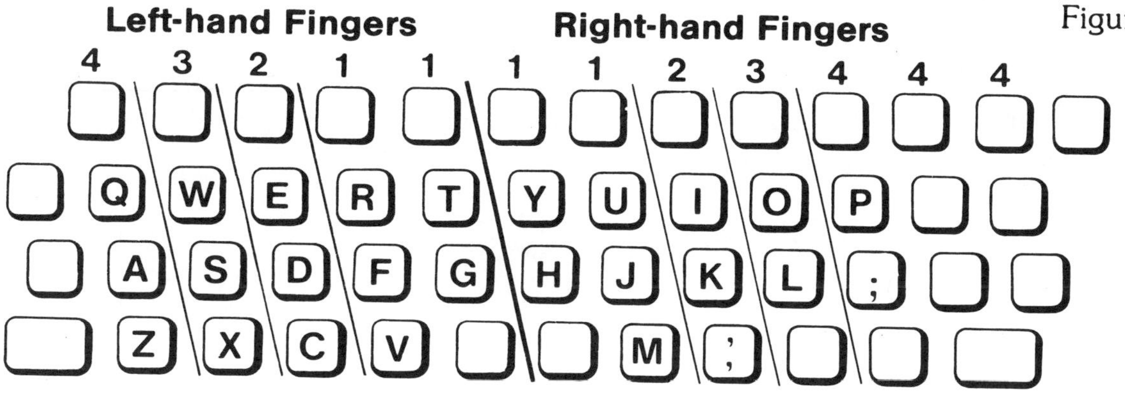

NEW KEYS M and Z

1. Locate the keys M and Z. Practise finger movements.
2. Keeping your eyes on the copy, type the following exercise **once.**

Exercise II

```
jmj jmj jmj jmj jmj jmj jmj jmj aza aza aza aza aza aza aza aza
```

3. Type the exercise once more. Concentrate on rhythmic movements and make sure that you are tucking your fingers **under** to reach the new keys.
4. Following instructions and reminders given in paragraph 3 (Revision) type the following exercise:

Exercise III

```
jjj mmm jmj jmj jjj mmm jmj jmj jjj mmm jmj jmj jjj mmm jmj jmj
me, me, my, my, am, am, him him me, me, my, my, am, am, him him
arm arm jem jem jam jam mow, mow, mite mite mate mate make make
most mist meat meet roam ream room time tame team terms, shames
aaa zzz aza aza aaa zzz aza aza aaa zzz aza aza aaa zzz aza aza
zoos zoos zeal zeal zest zest zoos zoos zeal zeal zest zest zip
ooze ooze haze haze gaze gaze laze laze maze maze jazz jazz zoo
```

5. Check your work. If necessary, carry out improvement practice (Lesson 4).

MEMORANDA

Informal letters used as communication between branches or departments of an organization are normally typed on printed memo forms (A4 or A5) and do not include a salutation or complimentary close.

MEMORANDUM

From	Head of Business & General Studies	***Ref***	HOD/PWM-18
To	All Course Tutors	***Date***	11 May 19..

Visit of BHC Personnel Officer

Mr Nigel Johnson will be visiting the College on Monday 1 June to talk to prospective trainees and to answer any questions they wish to ask about BHC.

Please submit the names of interested students to John Rice by Wednesday 17 May and ask those involved to notify lecturers, in advance, that they will be unable to attend classes after 2.15 pm.

Exercises:

1. Make 3 memo forms on **bond** paper, as follows:
   a) Insert A5 paper and carbons into the machine.
   b) Turn up 4 line spaces and type 'MEMORANDUM' 1 inch (25 mm) from the left.
   c) Turn up 3 line spaces and type 'From' at the left margin and 'Ref' at 58 (Elite) or 48 (Pica).
   d) Turn up 2 line spaces and type 'To' at the margin and 'Date' in line with 'Ref'.
2. Type a copy of the above memo, using a left margin of 1 inch (25 mm) (in line with headings) and a right of ½ inch (13 mm).
3. Type a second copy, but this time include 'standard' punctuation.
4. Compose a reply to the memo, listing 12 names in 3 columns (see fully-blocked letters with display matter).

Figure 21

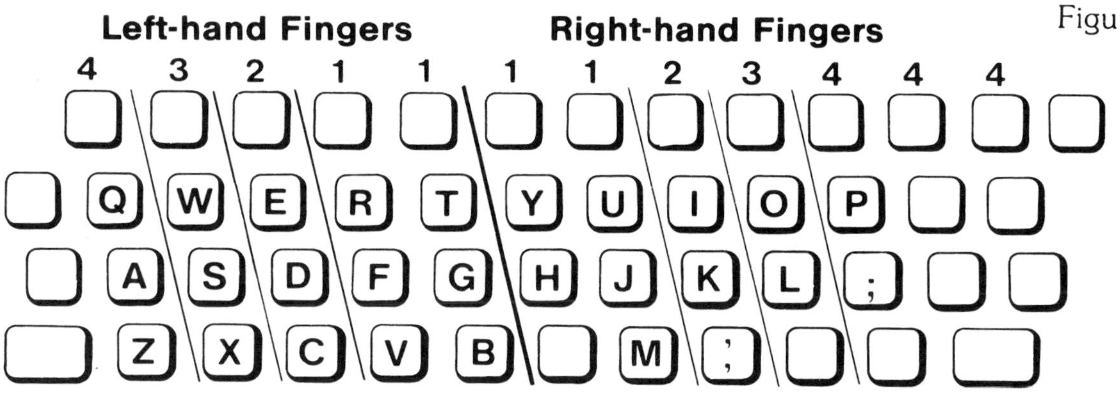

NEW KEY B

1. Locate the B key. Practise finger movements.
2. Keeping your eyes on the copy, type the following exercise **once.**

Exercise IV

```
fbf fbf fbf fbf fbf fbf fbf fbf
```

3. Type the exercise once more. Concentrate on rhythmic movements.
4. Following instructions given in paragraph 3 (Revision), type the following exercise:

Exercise V

```
fff bbb fbf fbf fff bbb fbf fbf fff bbb fbf fbf fff bbb fbf fbf

big big bad bad bat bat bet bet big big bad bad bat bat bet bet

but but bay bay boy boy buy buy lob lob cob cob sob sob fob fob

jab cab rib web gab jib be, box, base best boys bait beet beat;
```

5. Check your work. If necessary, carry out improvement practice (Lesson 4).

CONSOLIDATION

1. Type each of the following lines **three times,** trying to speed up a little when typing the line for the third time.

Exercise VI

```
graze craze dozes merry amaze alarm bloom broom boxes limbs climbs;

the child amazed us; his limbs were very small; he climbed the stairs;

please stop the alarm clock; he was merry as it was his birthday;

by tomorrow you will be able to type all the letters of the alphabet;
```

2. Check your work. If you have more than two errors in the **final** typing, carry out improvement practice (Lesson 4).

Exercises:

1. Type a copy of example (a) on A5 paper using 1 inch (25 mm) margins. (Turn up 2 spaces before and after the **attention line** and **subject heading**.)
2. Type a copy of the fully-blocked letter with a tear-off slip (example b) on A4 paper using 1 inch (25 mm) margins – allowing 1½ inches (38 mm) for heading. (Use the hyphen to indicate the tear-off line.)
3. Type a copy of example (c) on A4 paper using 1 inch (25 mm) margins – take 2 carbon copies. (Allow 1½ inches (38 mm) for heading.)
4. Type letter (a) in the fully-blocked form with 'open' punctuation, making all necessary changes in layout.
5. Type envelopes for all letters – including the attention lines **above** the address, as shown in the following example.

d) For the attention of Mr. J. Farmer

Hempstead Office Supplies Ltd.,
2, Buckingham Road,
KIDDERMINSTER,
Worcestershire.
KO31 6PG

CONTINUATION SHEETS

Long letters may require a second (continuation) sheet. In this case, plain paper is used and the name of the addressee, page number and date, typed at the top of the sheet.

In fully-blocked letters all details are typed at the left margin in **double-line** spacing (beginning on the fourth line) as follows:

('Open' style.)	**OR**	('Standard' style.)
2		-2-
18 January 19..		18th January, 19..
Messrs Edwards & Baker		Messrs. Edwards & Baker

In semi-blocked letters all details are typed on the fourth line as follows:

Messrs. Edwards & Baker	-2-	18th January, 19..

In both styles three spaces are turned up before the letter is continued.

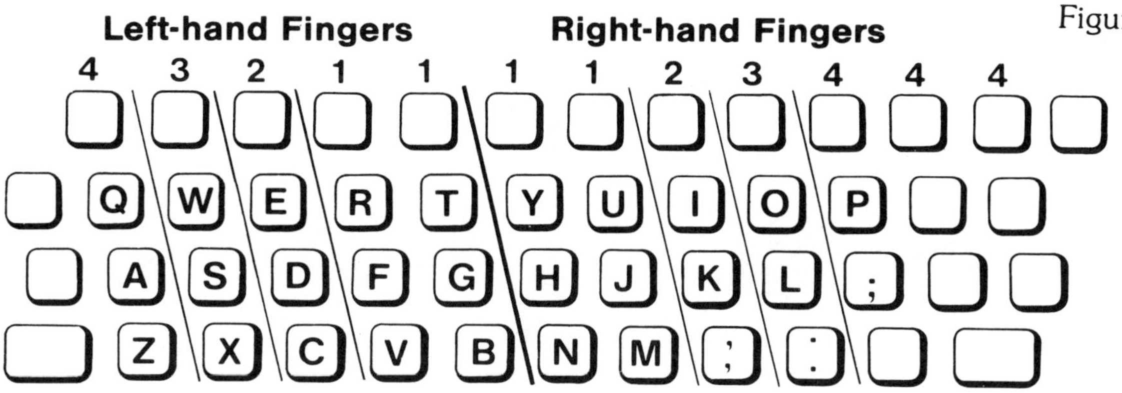

Figure 22

LESSON 12

REVISION

1. Insert paper into the machine. Set left margin stop at 18 (Elite) or 10 (Pica) and the line-space regulator on single-line spacing.
2. Prepare to type.
3. Type each of the following lines **three times,** leaving one line-space between each set of three. **Remember to: Keep your eyes on the copy; check your work at the end of the exercise only.**

Exercise I

```
but mat buy my, me, meat laze amaze craze broom boxes hover voices;

be a good girl, too little came of it, too much has become possible

this may be the time to go; lambs are with their mothers, have a care;

there is the exit, the colour is azure blue, play this game with us;
```

4. Repeat any lines you found to be difficult, taking care to move **fingers only** when you reach for keys.

NEW KEYS N and full stop (.)

1. Locate the keys N and full stop. Practise finger movements.
2. Keeping your eyes on the copy, type the following exercise **once.**

Exercise II

```
jnj jnj jnj jnj jnj jnj jnj jnj l.l l.l l.l l.l l.l l.l l.l l.l
```

3. Type the exercise once more. Concentrate on rhythmic movements.

(c)

PROCTOR CATERING SUPPLIES
SOUTH CROSS STREET
GOSPORT HANTS
PO20 4KT

Telephone
Gosport 26765

Telex
614397

Your Ref. QUO.GH/HR

18th June, 19..

Southern Hotels Ltd.,
24, Bedford Square,
Southampton.
SO34 5PJ

For the attention of Mr. J. Burgess

Dear Sirs,

Catering Cookers

Further to my visit to the Gurnard Hotel, I confirm that my recommendations for suitable cookers for the restaurant kitchen are as follows:

(i) Lawrence, Model 1833 - 4-ring hotplate, large griddle and double oven £712.00
Optional wall grill to match £187.00

(ii) Carlton, Model C12 - 6-ring hotplate and single oven with double doors £512.00
Optional wall grill to match £103.00

(iii) Black & Richards, Model 144/3 - 6-ring hotplate and single oven with double doors (complete with integral full-width grill) £1136.00

The prices quoted above are exclusive of VAT. The additional cost of fixing to the existing cooker position will be £34.00, plus VAT.

As you will see from the enclosed leaflets, all three are equally suitable for the proposed situation and fill all requirements outlined by the chef.

If you need any further information, please do not hesitate to contact me.

I look forward to receiving your order.

Yours faithfully,
PROCTOR CATERING SUPPLIES

J. Campbell
Sales Manager

Encs.

4. Following instructions and reminders given in paragraph 3 (Revision) type the following exercise:

Exercise III

```
jjj nnn jnj jnj jjj nnn jnj jnj jjj nnn jnj jnj jjj nnn jnj jnj

in, in, on, on, no, no, not not in, in, on, on, no, no, not not

nut nut net net now now man man pin pin tin tin pan pan tan tan

sun son hen send bend tend lend pend wend wind kind sand lands;

lll ... l.l l.l lll ... l.l l.l lll ... l.l l.l lll ... l.l l.l
```

5. Take the paper out of the machine and look at the back to see if the full stops are showing as heavy indentations or even holes! If so, practise the last line, giving less touch on the full stop, until the impression is much lighter.

6. Check the rest of your work. If necessary, carry out improvement practice (Lesson 4).

Note: There will be more work on the full stop in Lesson 15 – after you have learned to operate the Shift Keys (Figure 23).

CONSOLIDATION

1. Work through the following exercises, typing each of the lines **three times,** speeding up a little when typing the line for the third time. Check your work at the end of each **exercise.** If you have more than two errors in the **final** typing, carry out improvement practice (Lesson 4). **Remember to take a break when tired.**

Exercise IV

```
knib know knew knot knit kneel knight under, hinder rewind wren

round refine found sound print sprint depend pretend knowledge;

ping spring thing owing blowing towing happening fishing lowing
```

Exercise V

```
mother, father, sister, brother, uncle, aunt, cousin, friend.

relate, relates related relation protect protects protection.

exhibit exhibition expect, expects expectation miss missions.

press depress depression relax relaxed realize realization in
```

Exercise VI

```
have having give giving see seeing make making hope hoping, quiz.

me meeting go going do doing fast fastening happen happening; no.

that is the end of the line; kick the tin can; that cannot be so.

jump for joy, you look happy, make a step forward, take it from me.
```

(b)

THE ALBANY GUEST HOUSE
Nr Lymington
Hants SO7 2BA

Proprietors: V & J Morrison Telephone: Lymington 1234

---

12 February 19..

Mr K Abraham
14 South View Road
Winchester
W12 1TP

Dear Mr Abraham

Thank you for your letter of 7 February, asking for our brochure and tariff.

As you will see from the enclosed illustrated brochure, the Albany is a large, beautifully appointed Country House on the edge of the New Forest; an ideal spot for a relaxing break at any time of the year.

The prices quoted below are for Dinner, Bed and Breakfast per person, inclusive of VAT.

	Daily	Weekly
Single room without bathroom	£15.00	£98.00
Twin-bedded room without bathroom	£14.00	£91.00
Twin-bedded room with private bathroom	£15.00	£98.00

To reserve accommodation, please return the attached form or telephone your booking and send the form as confirmation.

We shall be pleased to give you any further information and hope to have the pleasure of welcoming you to the Albany in the very near future.

Yours sincerely

Enc

- -

Name .... Address ....

Please reserve ..... single/double* room(s) with/without* private bathroom for

..... days from .... to ....

I enclose a deposit of £..... (£1 per person, per day).

Cheque/PO* No ....

* Please delete where inapplicable.

LESSON 13

REVISION

1. Insert paper into the machine. Set the left margin at 12 or 10 (1 inch or 25 mm) and the line-space regulator on single-line spacing.
2. Prepare to type.
3. Paying special attention to the correct spacing between the **short** words, type the following exercise, containing over sixty of the most commonly used words, **once** only.

Exercise I

```
a of to in we is be on it as or at by if us an in me do so no up

the and you for are our not all has any one was may new but now;

your that will this have with very from they dear been time year

yours which truly would order these please their there other out
```

4. Practise the words you found to be difficult and then retype the exercise.

Note: If you have developed any of the typing faults outlined in Lesson 1, or find that 'dropped', 'raised' or 'crammed' letters are appearing in your typing, you should use the rest of this lesson to try to master the technique of 'rhythm' in order to eliminate faults and produce **even** typing. Instead of attempting Accuracy/Speed Building which will possibly increase your faults, use the time available to carry out revision on Lessons 8-12. Use Lesson 7 as a guide and **pay special attention to reminders.**

ACCURACY/SPEED BUILDING

Now that you are able to type the complete alphabet, you must concentrate on building both accuracy and speed.

1. The procedure for accuracy/speed building exercises in this and future lessons will be as follows:
   a) Check **before** you begin to type that posture and hand positions are correct and that you have enough line spaces to complete the exercise.
   b) Type each line three times – the third as fast as possible.
   c) Check your work at the end of each **exercise** only.
   d) Carry out improvement practice if you have more than two errors in the **final** typing.
2. Type the following exercises as instructed above. **Remember to take a break when tired.**

Exercise II

```
a an and are area answer all also at attend add advance as assist

be been bow bowl bet better bit bitter bend bent beer bear bearer

cod code coal coat coated cite cited city car care cares caring;
```

SECTION 2

BUSINESS LETTERS

The following examples of fully-blocked and semi-blocked (indented style) letters include attention lines, subject headings and display paragraphs. When typing display material within a fully-blocked letter (example b) it should be typed at the margin, but within a semi-blocked (example c), the longest line should be centred on the typing line. In the semi-blocked style, subject headings should also be centred and the complimentary close either centred (example a) or started at the centre of the typing line (example c). It is usual to include standard punctuation in semi-blocked letters and to type the date on the right-hand side (optional for fully-blocked letters).

See exercises on page 74.

(a)

Ref. JF/BW   1st April, 19..

Hempstead Office Supplies Ltd.,
2, Buckingham Road,
Kidderminster,
Worcestershire.
KO31 6PG

For the attention of Mr. J. Farmer

Dear Sirs,

Our Order No. 85267

Thank you for your letter of 18th June, acknowledging receipt of the above order for bond and bank typing paper.

As already explained, our stock of bond paper is now very low and it is most important that we receive the paper within the 2 week delivery period quoted.

We trust you will give priority to this item.

Yours faithfully,
CHAPMAN & BROWN LTD.

H. Robertson
Purchasing Officer

Exercise III

do dot dotted dear deer date dated dare daring due duet die died

eve ever evil even event eventually ear earn earning ease easy

foe for fore fee few fir firm fear feared fun funny for former

Exercise IV

go got get give given giving glue glued gut gutted grow grower

he her him his has have haven halt halted here hear haunt haunted

it is in ink intend intended interest interesting ill illness ice

Exercise V

jag jagged joy joyous jam jammed jug judge judging jury jet jettison

kit kite kilt kilted knit knitting knot knotted knife knives kin kind

lie lied lay laid low lower lowered loud louder load loading late later

3. If time allows, type all lines (Exercises II – V) **once** more.

LESSON 14

ACCURACY/SPEED BUILDING

1. Using a 1 inch (25 mm) left margin and single-line spacing, work through the following exercises proceeding as for Lesson 13 (Accuracy/Speed Building). Take a break when tired.

Exercise I

me met meet meeting mere merge merger more moreover mourn mourning

no not note noted near nearer nearing noon noun none new news newer

on one owe owing own owner out outing outrage open opener openings

Exercise II

pea peat peace port pork pore pet petted park parked paint painting

queue queued quest question query queries quote quoted quotation

re rent rented run runner row rowed round rounder ring ringing

SPEED TEST (Target time 3 minutes – Errors allowed: one per minute)

1. Prepare to type Exercise IV in single-line spacing using margins of 20 and 85 or 10 and 75.

2. Set a timer or ask someone to time you for 3 minutes. If this is not possible, note the time before you begin, type the complete exercise and note the time when you finish.

Exercise IV

```
                         (5)                   (10)
Now that you have completed the course, you should try to
                  (15)                  (20)
build on your present speed and ability by typing from
              (25)                (30)
printed copy whenever possible.  The large-print books avail-
   (35)                (40)                  (45)
able from public libraries are particularly useful for copy

practice.

          (50)                (55)                  (60)
In the second section of this book you will find examples of
                 (65)                 (70)
layouts for specialized work which I hope will help you to
             (75)                (80)
achieve your specific typing needs.
```

3. Check your work for errors and calculate your speed by dividing the number of words typed (indicated by figures in brackets) by 3 to give the number of 'words per minute' you have typed for a period of 3 minutes, **or** divide the number of words by the number of minutes taken to complete the exercise, if you were not timed. (i.e. $80 \div 4 = 20$)

If you typed at 20 words per minute (or over) and had the minimum number of errors specified, you have made excellent progress. With practice both your speed and accuracy will improve. Why not set yourself a goal to improve your present speed by 10 words per minute during the **next** 30 days!

Figure 23

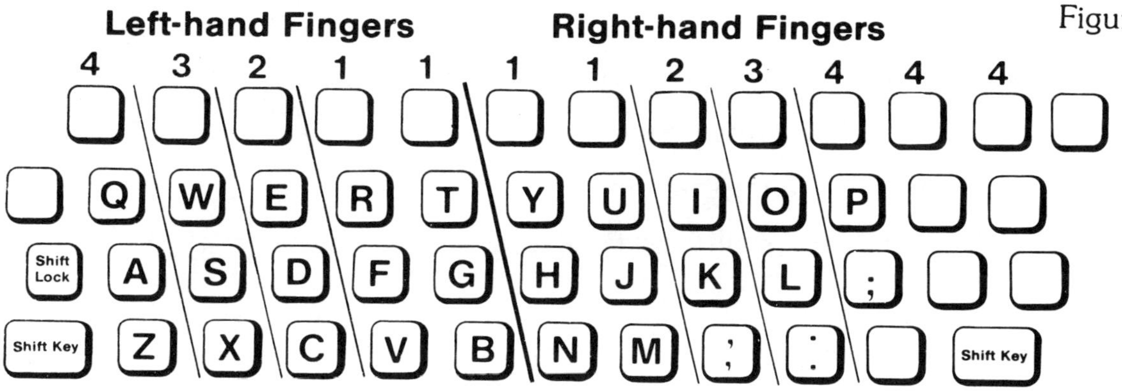

Exercise III

see seen sea seam so sow soon soonest show shower sun sunshine

to too two the then them they this these those their therm thermal

up upon unsaid under underneath understand utter uttered utterance

Exercise IV

via vial view viewed vale veil veiled vote voter vend vendor viz.

we were wear who whom why when what wise wiser wisdom won wonder

exotic exit exhibit exhibition exhaust exhausted exalt exaltation

Exercise V

you your yours youth yea yeast year yearn yearning yarn yarned yen

zone zoned zest zoo zoom zoomed azure amaze amazing zeal zealous

THE SHIFT KEYS

1. Locate the Shift Keys.
2. Push down the right shift key with your little finger (right). (You will probably have to **raise** other fingers above the home keys, but **do not** move your hand.) As you will see, when the shift key is depressed, the type basket is lowered (manual machines) causing the capital (upper case) letters to come into line with the PRINTING POINT(11) (Figure 1). Release the right shift key and return finger to home key.
3. Push down the left shift key with the little finger (left). Release the key and return finger to home key.
4. To type a capital letter – 'T' for instance – located on the left of the keyboard, the right-hand shift key must be operated as follows:

4. Begin to type Exercise II (without correcting) as follows:
   a) Type CROCUS, depress tabulator
   b) Type ALMOND, depress tabulator
   c) Type AZALEA, return the carriage, and so on.

Exercise II

CROCUS	ALMOND	AZALEA
DAFFODIL	CHERRY	BROOM
HYACINTH	CRAB APPLE	FORSYTHIA
TULIP	MAGNOLIA	BUDDLEIA
IRIS	PLUM	DEUTZIA

5. Check your work, paying special attention to the spacing.
6. Prepare Exercise III ready for typing in **double-line** spacing on A5 **landscape** paper. **Remember to allow for an extra space after the main heading, which should be typed at the margin.** (No extra space is required after the column headings.)
7. Type the following exercise, correcting typing errors where necessary; capitalise and underscore only where shown.

Exercise III

FORTHCOMING AUCTIONS (I.O.W.)

Property	Area	Month
Hotel	Bembridge	November
Boat Builders	Cowes	December
Guest House	Totland	January
Gift Shop	Sandown	February
Hotel	Ventnor	February

8. Check your work. Is the table centred both horizontally and vertically? Is the space between the columns equal? Have you corrected all typing errors?
9. If it is not a perfect copy, type the exercise once more.

Figure 24

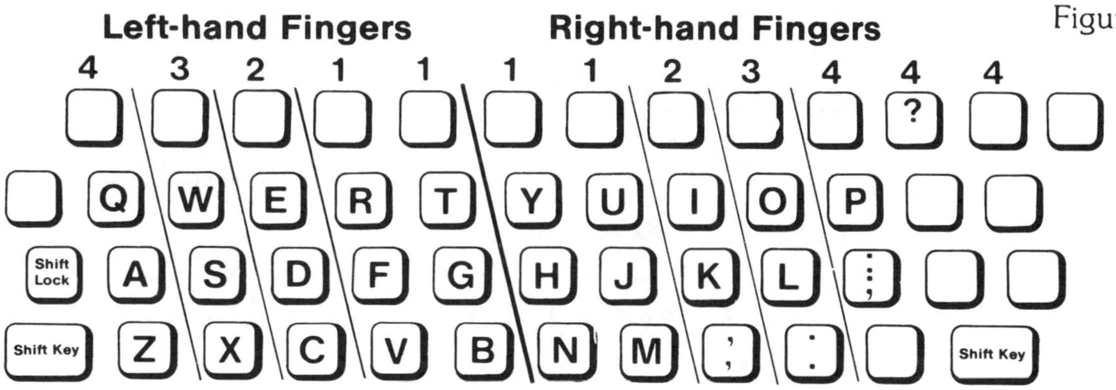

a) Depress the shift key and hold firmly in position.

b) Strike 'T' and return finger to home key.

c) Release shift key and return little finger to home key.

If these movements are rushed, 'raised' or 'lowered' capitals will appear in your work (manual machines). Practise movements a - c until you can carry them out without looking at the keyboard.

5. Practise typing the word 'Row' for a complete line, as follows:

a) Depress shift key (right).
b) Strike 'R'.
c) Return 1st finger to home key.
d) Release shift key.
e) Return little finger to home key.
f) Type 'o w', space.

6. Practise in the same way the word 'Page', using the left shift key. You will find it helpful to say to yourself: "Shift down 'P', release, 'a g e' space". (On the word 'release', fingers operating both 'P' and shift key are returned to home keys.)

CONSOLIDATION

1. Type the following exercise **once** only.

Exercise VI

```
Dartford, Winchester, Fulham and Gravesend need the right shift key.
Operate the left shift key for London, Hayes, York and Manchester.
```

2. Check your work. If any capital letters are 'raised', practise the operation of the shift keys before typing the exercise once more.

LESSON 15

PUNCTUATION

In previous lessons you have been leaving **one** character space after typing a comma or semi-colon. **One** space is also left after a colon. At the end of a sentence – whether finishing with a full stop, question mark or exclamation mark – **two** spaces are left as in Exercise I (tap the space bar twice). When the full stop is used after an abbreviation such as Mr. (Exercise I – line 4), or after an initial (Exercise III – line 3), **one** space only is left before typing the following word.

Exercise I

The Abbeyfield Squash Club

D I S C O (Spaced Caps.)

will be held at the

REGENTS HALL (Closed Caps.)

on Friday 8th December

at 8.30 p.m.

Price, including supper: £2.50

All members and guests welcome

3. Check your work to see if each line is in fact central.

TABULATION

Tables (items arranged in columns) must also be centred both horizontally and vertically on the paper.

1. Exercise II is to be typed in **double-line** spacing on A5 (portrait) paper. To arrive at the horizontal placement (margins) and the points at which to set tab stops for the columns you should proceed as follows:

   a) Count the number of character spaces needed for each column – calculated on the longest word in the column – and pencil in the figures above CROCUS, ALMOND, AZALEA.

   b) Add the figures together – allowing for 3 spaces between each column – to assess the total number of spaces contained in the width of the table.

   c) Divide the total by 2 and deduct that figure from the centre of the paper. Set the left margin stop at this point.

   d) Work out where to set tab stops for each column by adding the number of character spaces needed for column one, plus 3 spaces, to the left-hand margin (tab stop one). Continue by adding the number of spaces needed for column 2, plus 3 spaces to arrive at the point at which the second tab stop should be set.

2. Work out the vertical placement – as for the previous exercise – and turn up the appropriate number of spaces.

3. If your calculations are correct you will have set the left margin stop at 19 (Elite) or 13 (Pica); tab stops at 30 and 43 (Elite) or 24 and 37 (Pica); turned up 21 line-spaces (leaving 20 line-spaces for the top margin).

REVISION

1. Using a left margin of 1 inch (25 mm) and single-line spacing, type on A4 paper the following lines **once** only.

Exercise I

```
Mother is good.  John is very lovable.  Harold likes to swim.

Father works hard.  Dick and Susan have posted a letter to Chris.

Father and Mother questioned George about his outing to Warwick.

If you see Lucy, please give her my message.  Mr. Edwards is here.
```

2. Check your work. Is the spacing correct? Are all capitals in line? Are full stops light? If any capitals are 'raised', practise the operation of the shift key (Lesson 14).
3. Type the exercise **once** more. **Remember to: use a light touch on the full stop; keep your eyes on the copy when operating the shift key.**

NEW KEYS – Colon and Question Mark (: ?)

1. Locate the colon (Fig. 24). As you will see, it appears above the semi-colon and you therefore need to depress the shift key in order to type the colon.
2. Keeping your eyes on the copy and paying attention to rhythmic movements, type the following exercise **once** only.

Exercise II

```
:p; :p; :p; :p; :p; :p; :p; :p; :p; :p; :p; :p; :p; :p; :p; :p;
```

3. Type the following exercise **once** only.

Exercise III

```
Colours available are: Brown, Blue, Red and Green.

Delivery period: Four weeks from date of order.

The names are: P. Curry, S. Peach, L. Smith and D. Warren.
```

4. Check your work. Have you used the correct spacing after punctuation?
5. Type the exercise **once** more.
6. Locate the question mark. (On your machine it may not be in the position shown in Fig. 24). Once again, the shift key must be depressed in order to type the question mark. If the question mark is positioned above the comma, the 'K' finger must be used for operation (see line 2 Exercise IV). All keys situated to the right of the basic keyboard must be operated with the little finger.
7. Type either line one or line two (Exercise IV) **once** only. **Remember to: keep your eyes on the copy; listen to 'rhythm'; reach for keys without moving hands.**

Note: An alternative method of centring is to take the printing point to the centre of the typing line and depress the back-space key once for every 2 letters (and spaces) contained in the heading.

2. Using A4 paper, practise typing the headings shown above. Type them first assuming that the typing line to be used has **even** margins of 30 and 70 (Elite), 16 and 66 (Pica) and then in the correct position over **uneven** margins of your own choosing, bearing in mind that the left margin should be wider than the right. Before you type the headings, type a full stop at the selected margin points so that you will be able to measure the space either side of the heading to establish that the placement is in fact central between the two points. (If the figure to be divided was not an **even** number, there will of course, be a little more space on the **left** side of the heading.)

3. If time allows, type paragraphs under 'Centring a Heading' (1), to keep for reference.

   Note: In Section 2 you will find more examples of work using headings.

LESSON 30

VERTICAL CENTRING

In the last lesson you learned how to centre horizontally (Centring a Heading). To be able to type the following notice, which should be centrally positioned on the paper, you must also learn how to centre vertically.

1. Study Exercise I. As you will see, it contains 8 lines, but when typed in double-line spacing, it will in fact take up 15 typing lines. You know that 6 lines of type are equal to 1 inch (25 mm) and can therefore calculate that A5 portrait paper contains 50 lines. By deducting 15 from 50 you will see that you have left 35 lines to divide between top and bottom margins (17 above and 18 below). This exercise will therefore begin on line 18 (leaving 17 lines above the notice).

2. Type the following exercise on A5 (portrait) paper in **double-line** spacing, centring each line horizontally and the whole vertically. Before you begin:

   a) find the centre point of the paper by inserting it in the machine at '0' to check the number of character spaces portrait paper contains (shown on the paper scale) and dividing that figure by 2.

   b) calculate the points at which each line should begin and mark in pencil the appropriate figure beside each line– i.e. line one should be marked with the figure 22 (Elite) or 16 (Pica).

Exercise IV

```
;p? ;p? ;p? ;p? ;p? ;p? ;p? ;p? ;p? ;p? ;p? ;p? ;p? ;p? ;p? ;p?

k?k k?k k?k k?k k?k k?k k?k k?k k?k k?k k?k k?k k?k k?k k?k k?k
```

8. Type the following exercise **once** only. **Remember to leave two spaces after the question mark.**

Exercise V

```
Where is it?  What is the time?  Have you been to France?

Do you enjoy typewriting?  What is your speed?  May I?

Do you like poetry?  How old are you?  Are you there?
```

9. Check your work. Carry out improvement practice.
10. Type the exercise once more.

CONSOLIDATION

1. Type the following exercise **once** only.

Exercise VI

```
Can you type?  Is it difficult to learn?  How long will it take?

We have quoted for: one dozen, two dozen, six dozen and one gross.

What are your hobbies?  Can you swim?  When shall we meet?
```

2. Check your work, paying particular attention to correct spacing.
3. Type the exercise once more.

LESSON 16

ACCURACY/SPEED BUILDING

1. Proceed as for previous accuracy/speed building exercises, using a 1 inch (25 mm) left margin and single-line spacing.

Exercise I

```
I may have a new dress for the party.

You are coming to stay with us.

Father will be arriving tomorrow morning.

The end of the day has come.

When does your train arrive?
```

SETTING MARGIN AND TAB STOP	To avoid the use of the tabulator on every line, it is much easier when typing side headings, to set the margin stop at the beginning of the paragraph - for this exercise at 29 or 27 - and use the margin release to bring the typing point to 12 or 10 (1" margin) whenever a heading has to be typed. (Set a tab stop at this point.)

MAIN AND SUB-HEADINGS

Main headings may be be typed in closed capitals, with or without underscore (examples 1 and 2), in spaced capitals (example 3), or initial capitals with underscore (example 4). (When typing **spaced** capitals, three spaces are left between words.)

1) THE COLLINSON EXPERIMENT

2) TYPING "KNOW HOW"

3) T H E   F I R S T   A S S I G N M E N T

4) Childrens' Handicrafts

Sub-headings (headings typed immediately after a main heading) are normally typed with initial capitals (example 4) when following a main heading typed in closed capitals (examples 1 and 2) or in closed capitals when following a main heading typed in spaced capitals (example 3).

Both headings are normally placed at the centre of the typing line when indented paragraphs are used, or blocked at the margin when blocked paragraphs are appropriate. Two single-line spaces are left after a main heading standing alone (i.e. turn up 3 single-line spaces). When a sub-heading follows the main heading, one space is left after the main heading (i.e. turn up 2) and 2 spaces after the sub-heading (i.e. turn up 3). Note: When typing headings over work to be done in double-line spacing, always begin with the line-space lever on single-line spacing and change to double-line spacing when the 'body' of the work is reached.

CENTRING A HEADING

1. In order to centre a heading you must
   a) determine the centre point of the typing line
   b) count the number of character spaces contained in the heading you are about to type, divide the number by 2 and deduct that figure from the centre point.

When using **even** margins on A4 paper which has 100 character spaces (Elite) or 82 (Pica), you will know that the centre point of the typing line is 50 (Elite) or 41 (Pica). If however, **uneven** margins are being used, these must be added together and divided by 2 in order to establish the centre of the typing line (e.g. margins of 25 and 85 added together = 110 – the centre point would therefore be 55).

Example of centring on A4 paper using **even** margins:

The heading CAPITAL LETTERS has 15 characters (including the space between the words) and when divided by 2, equals 7½ spaces. Seven would therefore be deducted from the centre point (50 or 41) which means that the heading would begin at 43 on the paper scale (Elite) or 34 (Pica).

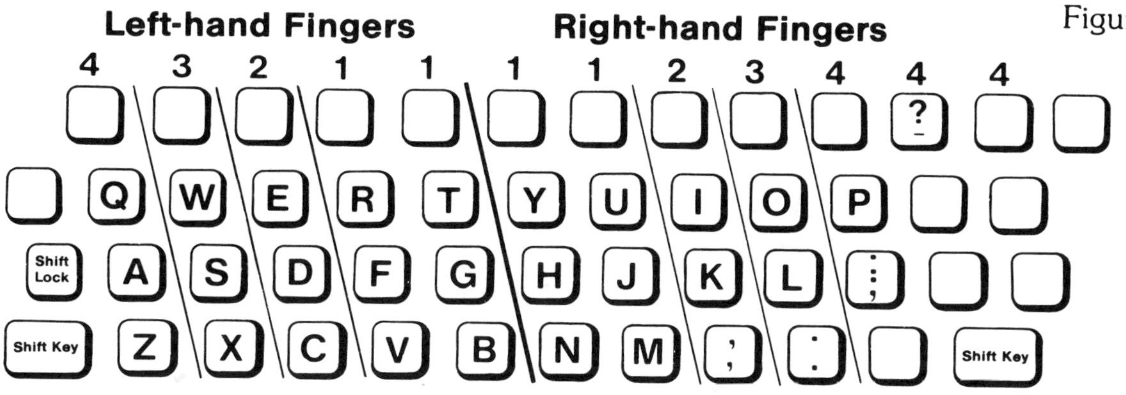

Figure 25

SPEED TEST (Target time: 1½ minutes – Errors allowed: 2)

1. Type Exercise I straight through **once,** keeping line-endings exactly as shown.
2. Check your work.
3. If you did not finish within the target time, type the exercise once more, making sure that you waste no time when returning the carriage. **Remember to: keep your eyes on the copy from beginning to end of exercise; return the carriage promptly.**

NEW KEYS – Hyphen/Dash (-)

1. Locate the hyphen/dash key. (It may not be in the exact position shown above.) Practise stretching the little finger to reach the top row, keeping other fingers over the home keys.
2. Keeping your eyes on the copy and paying attention to rhythmic movements, type the following exercise **once** only.

Exercise II

```
;p- ;p- ;p- ;p- ;p- ;p- ;p- ;p- ;p- ;p- ;p- ;p- ;p- ;p- ;p- ;p- ;p-
```

3. Study Exercise III. As you will see, when the character is used as a hyphen (lines 1 and 2), no space is left either side. When used as a dash (lines 4 and 5), one space is left **before** and **after** the character.
4. Type the following exercise **once** only.

Exercise III

```
line-end, one-third, daughter-in-law, full-time, left-hand.

first-class, second-hand, matter-of-fact, novel-writing.

I learned to type - using my own machine - accurately and neatly.

It could be weeks - or even months - before she is well once more.
```

5. Check your work. Practise any words/lines you found to be difficult.
6. Type the exercise once more.

7. Compose information to complete the form. (The signature space must be completed in ink.) **Remember to use double-line spacing.**
8. Complete the carbon copy using personal details.
9. If time allows, type a copy of paragraphs 3 – 6 and keep for reference.

LESSON 29

TYPES OF HEADING

The following exercises explain the layout of the three different types of heading used for sub-division under a main heading.

1. Read each exercise **before typing** on A5 (landscape) paper using 1 inch (25 mm) margins. Change line-endings as necessary and correct any errors made. (Keep the exercises for reference.)

Exercise I (Paragraph Headings)

Paragraph Headings. These may be typed in lower case letters with initial capitals and underscored, as for this paragraph, or in capitals without underscore.

Paragraph headings sometimes form part of the sentence, as in this paragraph and therefore need no punctuation after the heading. They may be typed at the margin (as in this blocked exercise) or begin 5 spaces from the margin when indented paragraphs are used.

Exercise II (Shoulder Headings)

SHOULDER HEADINGS

These headings are normally typed in capitals and may be underscored if preferred. The modern method is to leave out the underscoring in order to save time.

CORRECT POSITIONING

Shoulder headings are always typed at the margin, one clear space above the paragraph (i.e. turn up 2 spaces after the heading). They are never indented, although indented paragraphs may be used under a shoulder heading.

Exercise III (Side Headings)

SIDE HEADINGS	The headings in this exercise, sometimes called 'marginal' are used mainly for plays and sometimes for itineraries, minutes and specifications.
PLACEMENT	Side headings begin at the margin - for this exercise 1" from the left. Three character spaces should be left between the longest heading and the commencement of the paragraph.

continued over

Figure 26

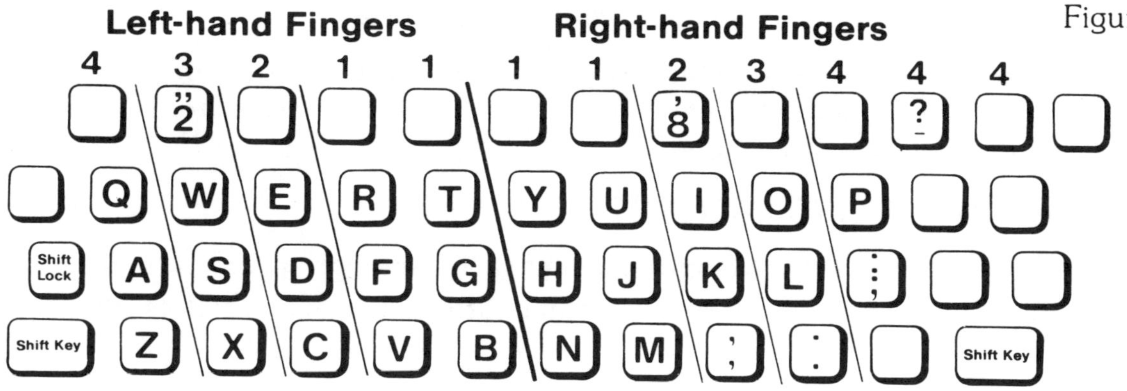

CONSOLIDATION

1. Type the following exercise **once** only.

Exercise IV

```
We will employ you on a full-time basis.  Part-time is offered.

Have you read his latest novel?  I have a paper-back copy.

The book - given to me by my father-in-law - has proved useful.
```

2. Check your work, paying particular attention to correct spacing.
3. Type the exercise **twice** more – the second as fast as possible.

LESSON 17

REVISION

1. Using a left margin of 1 inch (25 mm) and single-line spacing, type the following exercise **once** only.

Exercise I

```
The book is a clearly-written guide to creative writing.

Would you like to borrow my copy?  I am sure you will enjoy it.

The book covers: poetry, plays, novels, short stories.

The author says that you must be prepared to write daily.
```

2. Check your work, making sure that the spacing after punctuation is exactly as shown.
3. Type the exercise once more.

NEW KEYS – Figures 2 and 8 (upper case characters " and ')

1. Locate the figure 2 and practise stretching to reach the key. (Unless your hand/wrist positions are **correct,** you will find movements difficult.)

2. Erase the error on the top copy with a **hard** rubber.
3. Remove the card and erase the error on the carbon copy with a **soft** rubber. (When erasing **several** carbon copies, the card must be inserted in front of the second carbon copy before erasing the first and so on.)

MAKING AND FILLING-IN FORMS

Forms must be typed in double-line spacing to allow enough space for them to be filled in by hand or typewriter. When typing on an unbroken line or line of dots, all long letters (including commas) must appear just clear of the line. Example:

```
                           Hilary Pennington
Name (XX. Mrs. XXXX) ...........................................
```

1. Type the following form on A5 (landscape) paper using 1 inch (25 mm) margins Take one carbon copy. **Remember to: leave a top margin of 1 inch (25 mm); type dots lightly.**

Exercise II

```
Name (Mr. Mrs. Miss) ..............................................

Address ...........................................................

...................................................................

Previous employment ...............................................

...................................................................

Qualifications ....................................................

...................................................................

...................................................................

Date ...........................  Signature .......................
```

2. Remove the form from the typewriter and replace the **top copy only,** making sure that you line up correctly with the original margins and that the dots are in line with the alignment scale.
3. Delete the inapplicable courtesy titles (Mr. Mrs. Miss) by typing a capital X over each character you wish to delete (see example).
4. Prepare to complete the first line by lining up with the **last** typed character (bracket) and tapping 3 spaces on the space bar.
5. Turn back a half-space (turn cylinder knobs towards you) and complete the first line by inserting a name containing some long letters.
6. If the long letters are typed nearer or further away from the line than the example above, use the variable line-spacer to bring the type to the required position. Note: Once the first line is correctly placed, no further adjustment is needed for successive lines.

2. Keeping your eyes on the copy and paying attention to rhythmic movements, type the following exercise **once** only.

Exercise II

```
sw2 sw2 sw2 sw2 sw2 sw2 sw2 sw2 sw" sw" sw" sw" sw" sw" sw" sw"

s2s s2s s2s s2s s2s s2s s2s s2s s"s s"s s"s s"s s"s s"s s"s s"s
```

3. Type the following exercise **once** only.

Exercise III

```
I will see you on 2nd June.  Refer to figure 2 on page 2.

The sign " is used for inches.  Please draw a 2" square.

The sign " is also used for quotation marks.

"Please come here," said the boy.

"How are you?"  "I am very well, thank you."
```

4. Check your work. Practise any words/lines you found to be difficult.
5. Type another copy to keep for reference.
6. Locate the figure 8 and practise finger movements. (See Figure 26.)
7. Type the following exercise **once** only. **Remember to: keep your eyes on the copy; listen to 'rhythm'; stretch fingers to top row without moving your hand position.**

Exercise IV

```
ki8 ki8 ki8 ki8 ki8 ki8 ki8 ki8 ki' ki' ki' ki' ki' ki' ki' ki'

k8k k8k k8k k8k k8k k8k k8k k8k k'k k'k k'k k'k k'k k'k k'k k'k
```

8. Type the following exercise **once** only.

Exercise V

```
Will you please call on 8th August.  Refer to page 8.

The sign ' is used as an apostrophe.  The boy's pen.

The sign ' is used for feet.  The table is 8' long.

It is also used as a quotation mark and part of an exclamation mark.
```

9. Check your work and proceed as for 4 and 5 above.

CONSOLIDATION

1. Study the following exercise. As you will see, one space is left after the signs for feet and inches and either side of x (meaning by). A figure is **never** used at the beginning of a sentence (line 3).
2. Type the following exercise **once** only.

LESSON 28

CARBON COPYING

Organizations usually keep at least one copy of letters and business documents. This means that the typist must take a carbon copy on flimsy (bank) paper or make a photocopy.

1. To take one (A5) carbon copy of the next letter:

   a) Place the copy paper (bank) on the desk.
   b) On top of this – coated side down – place the carbon paper.
   (When additional copies are needed, steps (a) and (b) are repeated.)
   c) Place the typing paper (bond) on top of the carbon paper.
   d) Pick up all sheets by placing the thumbs underneath and fingers on top. (If the top edges are uneven, knock the top edges of the pack on the desk.)
   e) Insert the pack – top edges first – into the machine and adjust in the normal way.
   f) Check before typing, that the uncoated (decorative) side of the carbon paper is facing you.

2. Type the following business letter using 'standard' punctuation and 1 inch (25 mm) margins. **Do not** correct typing errors. Note that the name of the Company (KENT OFFICE SUPPLIES LTD.) is typed in capitals on the line following 'Yours faithfully'. Paragraph as necessary.

Exercise I

To:
Messrs R.P. Standard & Co., 14, Kent Street, Dartford, Kent.
DA1 4UJ
Dear Sirs, Thank you for your letter of 23rd March
requesting details of our range of office furniture. The
enclosed brochure and price list should give you all the
information you require, but if you feel we can be of
further assistance to you, please let us know. We look
forward to receiving your order. Yours faithfully,
KENT OFFICE SUPPLIES LTD.

3. Check your work, paying attention to layout and punctuation.

4. Type a second copy of the letter making corrections where necessary, to both the top and carbon copy, by following the instructions outlined below.

ERASING Carbon Copies (To be practised on manual machines only.)

1. Before erasing the top copy, insert a piece of card or paper between the carbon and copy paper, behind the error to be erased.

Figure 27

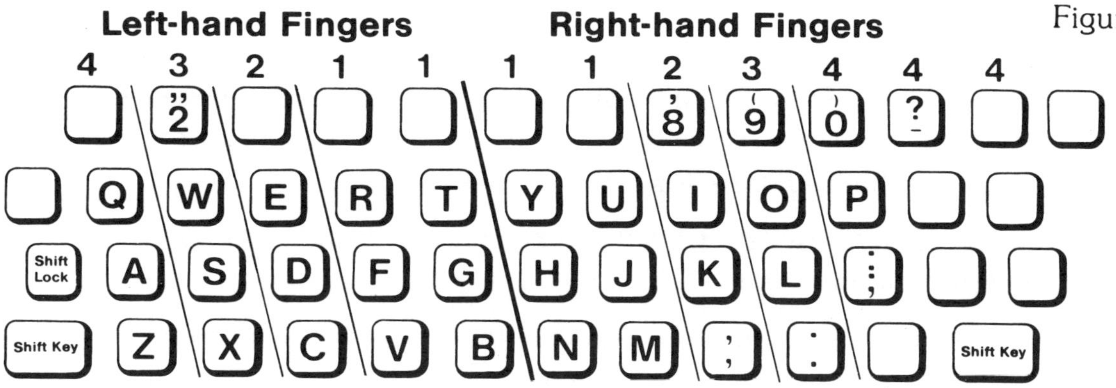

Exercise VI

The man's coat was brown. The girls' frocks were white.

The table is 2' 8" long and 2' 2" wide. The cupboard is 8' 2" x 8'.

Twelve of us attended the party given on 8th September.

It is outlined in Figure 2 on page number 28.

On the 8th line it says: "Are you going to accept this boy's view?".

"Please give me the book entitled 'For Pleasure'," said the girl.

3. Check your work, paying particular attention to correct spacing.
4. Type the exercise once more.

LESSON 18

REVISION

1. Using a left margin of 1 inch (25 mm) and **double-line spacing**, type the following exercise once only.

Exercise I

As the bus slowed down, Sue stood up.

"Are you going to buy some shoes at lunch-time?" I said.

"Yes, will you come with me?"

"I'll meet you outside your office just after one."

"Remember I have to be back by two o'clock," she called, jumping off.

2. Check your work, making sure that the spacing after punctuation is exactly as shown.
3. Type the exercise once more.
4. Change the line-space regulator to single-line spacing.

NEW KEYS – Figures 9 and 0 [upper case characters (and)]

1. Locate the figures 9 and 0 and practise finger movements. (If your typewriter does not have a figure 0, you must use an upper case 'o' (L finger) for Exercise III.

BUSINESS LETTERS

The following letter is a reply to the previous exercise (II). As it is a business letter it is typed on the Company's headed paper. The company concerned obviously prefer their typists to use the 'standard' form of punctuation.

1. Compare the business letter below with Exercise II and note the differences in puctuation.
2. Type a copy of the following letter on A5 paper in single-line spacing, using margins of 1 inch (25 mm). Leave a top margin of 1½ inches (38 mm) — space normally occupied by the printed heading. Note that this time punctuation is included in a.m.

Exercise III

THE PLANET INSURANCE COMPANY

20 HOVE ROAD

WELLING KENT

Telephone:
29657

Telex:
79601

a) Turn up 3 lines from end of heading – type date

7th October, 19..

Mrs. M. Constable,
24, The Terrace,
Dartford,
Kent.
DA1 1UJ

Dear Mrs. Constable,

I am sorry that I have been unable to call at your home for over 2 months, but this has been due to the fact that I have been confined to the office in the absence of our Area Manager.

Mr. Johnson has now recovered from his illness and I will be returning to the District next week. I hope to call on you around 11 a.m. on Wednesday.

Yours sincerely,

b) Turn up 5 lines (room for signature) – type name.

J. ROBERTS

3. Check your work, paying particular attention to spacing and punctuation.
4. If time allows, compose a reply to the letter to Mary (Exercise I). Use your home address and either 'open' or 'standard' punctuation.

2. Keeping your eyes on the copy and paying attention to rhythmic movements, type the following exercises **once** only.

Exercise II

```
lo9 lo9 lo9 lo9 lo9 lo9 lo9 lo9 lo( lo( lo( lo( lo( lo( lo( lo(

l9l l9l l9l l9l l9l l9l l9l l9l l(l l(l l(l l(l l(l l(l l(l l(l
```

Exercise III

```
;pO ;pO ;pO ;pO ;pO ;pO ;pO ;pO ;p) ;p) ;p) ;p) ;p) ;p) ;p) ;p)

;O; ;O; ;O; ;O; ;O; ;O; ;O; ;O; ;); ;); ;); ;); ;); ;); ;); ;);
```

Exercise IV

```
Look at number 9 on the list.  Refer also to item number 90.

Ninety (90) people attended the meeting.

No space is left before the closing bracket (character above 0).

No space is left after the opening bracket (character above 9).

One space is left before the opening bracket.

One space is left after the closing bracket, except when it is

followed by punctuation.
```

3. Check Exercise IV. Practise words/lines you found to be difficult.
4. Type another copy to keep for reference.

THE SHIFT LOCK

The Shift LOCK is situated above the left Shift KEY (Figure 27). This key is used to lock the shift keys in position in order to type several capital letters or to underscore words.

1. To type a word in capital letters the following procedure must be used:
   a) Depress the shift lock with the little finger (left hand).
   b) Return finger to home key.
   c) Type the word to be capitalised.
   d) Release the shift lock by depressing the left shift KEY.
   e) Return finger to home key.
   f) Tap space bar and continue.
2. Type the following exercise **once** only. (No space is left between the full stops **within** the abbreviations B.B.C. and p.m.)

Exercise II

a) Turn up 4 lines before typing the address

24 The Terrace
Dartford
Kent
DA1 1UJ

b) Turn up 3 lines – type date

3 October 19..

c) Turn up 3 lines – type address

Mr J Roberts
The Planet Insurance Company
20 Hove Road
Welling
Kent
WE30 5LP

d) Turn up 3 lines – type salutation

Dear Mr Roberts

e) Turn up 2 lines – type body of letter

On checking my insurance payments book I find that it is nearly 3 months since you last called to collect my monthly premium.

As I do not like being in arrears, will you please call as soon as you can. I am always at home between 10 am and 2 pm.

f) Turn up 2 lines – type complimentary close.

Yours sincerely

4. Check your work.
5. Retype Exercise II, but before you begin, cover up the marginal instructions and memorize the spacing between the parts of the letter. Correct typing errors. **Remember to check the letter carefully before removing it from the machine.**

Exercise V

```
JOHN and PATRICIA live in BIRMINGHAM.

DAVID and YVONNE live in MANCHESTER.

The ANNUAL GENERAL MEETING is to be held on 9th June at 2 p.m.

The programme was recorded by the B.B.C. on 29th August.
```

3. Check your work. Practise any words/lines you found to be difficult.
4. Type the exercise once more.

CONSOLIDATION

1. Type the following exercise **once** only. **Remember to: make careful, precise movements; keep you eyes on the copy throughout the exercise.**

Exercise VI

```
Our membership is now 890 (eight hundred and ninety).

Item number 9 refers to members under the age of 20.

ALWAYS use the SHIFT LOCK when typing a word in U.C. (upper case).

Use the SHIFT KEY to type an INITIAL CAPITAL (first letter of a word).

ALWAYS use the SHIFT LOCK when underscoring.
```

2. Check your work. Carry out improvement practice where necessary.
3. If time allows, type the exercise once more.

LESSON 19

ACCURACY/SPEED BUILDING

1. Proceed as for previous accuracy/speed building exercises, using a 1 inch (25 mm) left hand margin and single-line spacing.

Exercise I

```
Any advanced ideas are always welcome.

Blue ribbons adorned her beautiful hair.

Carbon copies are required for this contract.

Do not delay delivery of the draft documents.
```

LESSON 27

PERSONAL LETTERS

The following is an example of a letter typed in the 'open' punctuated style. As you will see, no punctuation is inserted in the address, date, or after the salutation (Dear Mary). Normal punctuation is used within the body of the letter but no punctuation follows the complimentary close (Love).

1. Using A5 paper with the short edge at the top (portrait), type a copy of the following letter in single-line spacing, using 1 inch (25 mm) margins. Set a tab stop for the address at 45 (Elite) or 34 (Pica).

Exercise I

a) Turn up 4 lines before typing the address

```
                                Brookside
                                New Road
                                Porchfield
                                Newport
                                Isle of Wight
                                PO30 4LT
```

b) Turn up 3 lines – type date

```
                                1 October 19..
```

c) Turn up 3 lines – type salutation

```
Dear Mary
```

d) Turn up 2 lines – type paragraph one

```
It is ages since I heard from you.  I hope that
you and your family are well and enjoyed your
holiday in Devon.
```

e) Turn up 2 lines between paragraphs

```
Malcolm and I went to Scotland once again and
found it as beautiful as ever.  We have been
back just over a fortnight but I am still
reluctant to get down to work.

I hope you will be able to visit us for a week-
end this Autumn.  The children will enjoy walk-
ing in the woods and playing on the deserted
beaches.

Please write soon.
```

f) Turn up 2 lines – type complimentary close.

```
Love
```

2. Check your work, paying particular attention to the spacing.
3. Following instructions outlined in Paragraph 1, type the following more formal letter where the address of the **addressee** is also included. Note that no punctuation is included in the abbreviations a.m. and p.m.

Figure 28

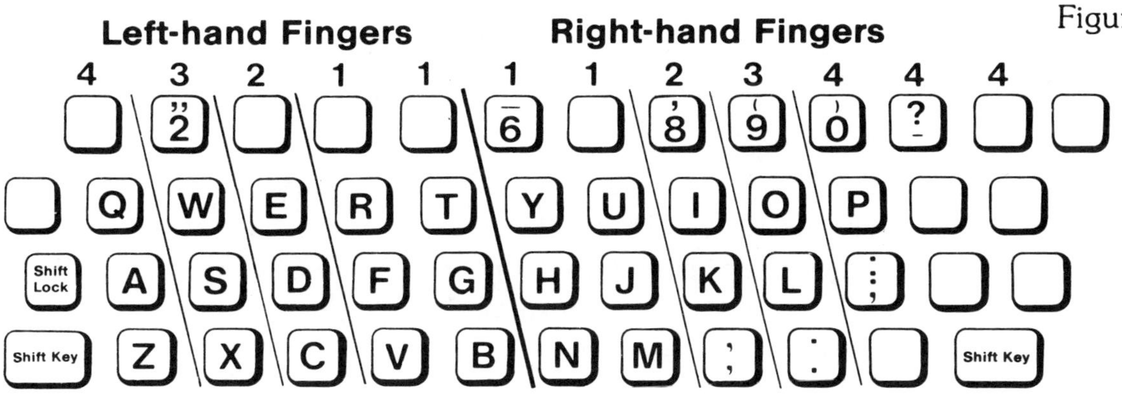

NEW KEY – Figure 6 (upper case character _)

1. Locate the figure 6 and underscore key. As you will see, it is a long reach from J to 6 and unless your fingers are in the correct position over the keys (see Before You Type Check . . .) you will not be able to strike the key correctly. (The movement from J to 6 may necessitate lifting more than one finger from the home keys, but make sure that the little finger is 'anchored' on its home key so that the other fingers may be returned with ease.) Practise finger movements.
2. Keeping you eyes on the copy and paying attention to rhythmic movements, type the following exercise **once** only.

Exercise II

```
ju6 ju6 ju6 ju6 ju6 ju6 ju6 ju6 ju_ ju_ ju_ ju_ ju_ ju_ ju_ ju_

j6j j6j j6j j6j j6j j6j j6j j6j j_j j_j j_j j_j j_j j_j j_j j_j
```

3. Type each of the following lines three times.

Exercise III

```
There were 6 boys at the party.  Please buy 6 fresh cream cakes.

Are you free on 6th June?  The next time I am free is 26th July.
```

4. Check your work. Carry out improvement practice where necessary.
5. The underscore key is used to draw a line under a word or words needing emphasis (Exercise IV). When it is necessary to underscore a word or phrase, the line of type must be **completed** before going back to underscore. Having reached the end of the typing line, the following procedure should be carried out:
   a) Using the carriage release levers (back-space key on electronic machines), guide the carriage/carrier back to the place where the printing point is in line with the first letter of the word to be underscored.
   b) Depress the shift LOCK and return finger to home key.
   c) Strike the underscore key once for each letter included in the word (letters **and spaces** in a phrase) and return to home key. **(Hold key down or use 'repeat' key - electronic machines.)**
   d) Release the shift lock and return to home key.
   e) Return the carriage.

1. Using A6 paper (A4 cut into four) type the above addresses in single-line spacing – punctuate where shown. Use a normal size backing sheet to assist in feeding the A6 paper round the cylinder.

Note: When typing a SPECIAL INSTRUCTION to the person opening the mail (e.g. CONFIDENTIAL), this must be typed in capitals one clear line space above the name of the addressee. When typing an instruction to the Post Office (e.g. FORCES AIR MAIL), this must also be typed in capitals at the left-hand margin about three spaces from the top of the envelope (opposite the stamp).

DATES

The two forms of date shown below are the **only** acceptable forms for letters. Example (a) is used when the letter is typed in the 'open' punctuated style and (b) when the letter is typed with 'standard' punctuation.

(a) 21 January 1989 (b) 21st January, 1989

6. Using the procedure outlined above, type the following exercise **once** only.

Exercise IV

Today's lesson, is in the main, information for you - the Typist.

Never underscore a punctuation mark which precedes or follows words

to be emphasised. When typing do not sacrifice accuracy to speed.

7. Check your work. Carry out improvement practice where necessary.
8. Type Exercise IV once more.

CONSOLIDATION

1. Read through the following exercise (the information refers to manual machines only), and then type it on a fresh sheet of A4 paper in **double-line** spacing. (Use a **black** ribbon throughout.)

   Set a 2 inch (51 mm) left margin (Elite) or 1 inch (25 mm) (Pica).

Exercise V

Use the SHIFT LOCK in order to type a perfect line.

If you use a black ribbon, underscoring will appear in black.

Is your machine fitted with a bi-chrome (red and black) ribbon?

If so, underscoring may also be done in red.

Somewhere near the keyboard you will find a ribbon-adjuster.

To type in red, the lever position must be set on 'red'.

After underscoring the lever must be returned to 'black'.

(The 'white' position is used when typing a stencil.)

Unless you will be using red regularly, buy an all black ribbon.

The black ribbon can be turned over when the top half is worn.

The bi-chrome is often thrown away half used.

2. Check your work. If it is inaccurate, type a further copy to keep for reference. If accurate, type it once more, trying to speed up on underscoring procedures (5a – e).

6. Check your work, paying special attention to layout.

7. Type another copy of Exercise II, but this time use **letters** instead of figures (see examples in paragraph 4 above) and **block** the display paragraphs (i.e. begin the second line of each lettered paragraph under the first **word** of the paragraph). Adjust line-endings and erase where necessary.

8. Check your work **before** removing it from the machine. Keep both attempts for reference. By comparing the two styles you will be able to decide on your personal preference of both layout and use of letters and figures.

ENVELOPES

When typing envelopes, the address should begin approximately half-way down and when using standard envelopes, 2 inches (51 mm) from the left-hand edge. (When larger envelopes are used, the left-hand margin should be adjusted accordingly.)

By studying the following examples you will notice that:

a) the TOWN is always typed in capitals

b) a courtesy title is used unless you are writing to a limited company (iii) **or** a company that has an 'impersonal' name (v), when 'The' is normally included in the title.

c) addresses may be typed with or without punctuation ('standard' or 'open' styles).

d) initials before the name have spaces between, but initials **after** (degrees) have no space left between them (iv).

(i) Messrs W J Biggs & Sons
45 Victoria Street
LUTON
Beds
LU1 0WS

(ii) Miss J Collinson
24 The Avenue
DARTFORD
Kent
DA2 1UJ

(iii) Smith & Brown Ltd
144-149 Bridge Street
LONDON
SE1 9PL

(iv) Mr. J. P. Collins, B.A.,
18, Juniper Street,
FRESHWATER,
Isle of Wight.
PO30 5LK

(v) The British Freight Co.,
Russel Wharf,
GRAVESEND,
Kent.
GU2 8EJ

(vi) Mr. & Mrs. J. B. Martin,
Hillside,
Sherwood Lane,
CAMBRIDGE.
CB1 4NP

LESSON 20

ACCURACY/SPEED BUILDING

1. Proceed as for previous accuracy/speed building exercises, using a 1 inch (25 mm) margin and single-line spacing.

Exercise I

```
Evening eating in exclusive restaurants has become a popular pastime.

Far too many people find fattening food preferable to nutritious food.

Graduates generally give willingly to this great cause.

Hundreds of horsemen assembled for the Heathfield Championships.
```

SPEED TEST (Target time: 1 minute – Errors allowed: one)

1. Type the following exercise once for practice and then once for speed.

Exercise II

```
A bad typist produces untidy work.

A good typist is both neat and accurate.

It is a pleasure to read a neatly presented typescript.
```

2. Check your work.
3. If you did not finish within the target time, type it once more. **Remember to: prepare to type with care; keep your eyes on the copy throughout the exercise; return the carriage/carrier promptly; keep your wrists and fingers loose.**

NEW KEYS – Figures 1 and 4 (upper case characters * and @)

Note: If there is not a figure one key on your machine, you must use a small "l" (home key). If the upper case characters on your typewriter are not in the same position as those shown in fig. 29 (p.44), write in the correct character - in the space provided above the key on the chart - and type it instead of the character given in the exercises that follow. (i.e. aq* should be replaced with aq!, if the exclamation mark appears above the figure 1 on your machine.)

1. Locate the figures 1 and 4 (Fig. 29) and practise finger movements.
2. Keeping your eyes on the copy and paying attention to rhythmic movements, type the following exercises **once** only.

Exercise III

```
aq1 aq1 aq1 aq1 aq1 aq1 aq1 aq1 aq* aq* aq* aq* aq* aq* aq* aq*

a1a a1a a1a a1a a1a a1a a1a a1a a*a a*a a*a a*a a*a a*a a*a a*a
```

Exercise IV

```
fr4 fr4 fr4 fr4 fr4 fr4 fr4 fr4 fr@ fr@ fr@ fr@ fr@ fr@ fr@ fr@

f4f f4f f4f f4f f4f f4f f4f f4f f@f f@f f@f f@f f@f f@f f@f f@f
```

2. Using A5 (landscape) paper, type the following exercise **once** in single-line spacing using margins of 20 and 84 (Elite) or 12 and 76 (Pica). Correct where necessary. N.B. **The information contained in exercises I & II refers to manual machines only.**

Exercise I

Your typewriter will have a longer life if it is cleaned after use and covered when not in use.

The type-faces of the machine should be brushed gently with a stiff brush and the rest of the machine with a soft brush.

Special attention should be given to the parts normally covered by the carriage. By using the carriage release to take the carriage to the extreme right or left, the underside becomes easily accessible.

Do not forget to clean underneath the typewriter and to dust all dirt from the desk.

3. Check your work **before** removing it from the machine. Keep for reference.

4. Study the numbered paragraphs in Exercise II (display work). As you will see, **two** character spaces are left after the full stop (not always included after figures). When figures **or** letters are followed by a bracket, two spaces are left after the bracket.

5. Type Exercise II **without correcting,** on A4 paper using single-line spacing and margins set for Exercise I. Set a tab stop **six** spaces from the left margin (position of second and subsequent lines of hanging 'display' paragraphs) . Adjust line-endings where necessary.

Exercise II

When you wish to make a neat correction, the eraser should be used as follows :

1. Turn the paper up to rest on the 'erasing table' (the metal strip above the cylinder) so that when you erase you will rub against metal and not the rubber cylinder.

2. Using the carriage release and margin release, take the carriage to the <u>extreme</u> left or right of the machine so that any rubber dust will fall on to the desk rather than into the machine. (The margin release must be <u>held down</u> in order to take the carriage to the extreme <u>right</u>.)

3. Holding the paper firmly with your left hand, take the eraser and rub carefully - using up and down movements - the letter(s) to be corrected. Blow away any dust that sticks to the paper.

4. Return the paper to its normal position (with paper bail down). Make sure that the printing point is in line with the erased letter(s) and type in the correct character(s).

With practice you will be able to make a correction which is not visible to the reader. NEVER erase over the typewriter or you will find that the abrasive dust which drops from the rubber will have a corrosive effect on your machine.

Exercise V

Come to stay on 11th April. Ask her to be there at 4 p.m.

Sally's party is on 14th May. Twenty are expected at 1, The Avenue.

3. Check Exercise V. Carry out improvement practice where necessary.
4. Type the exercise once more.

CONSOLIDATION

1. Read through the following exercise and then type it **once** in **double-line** spacing on a fresh sheet of A4 paper.

Exercise VI

When standing alone, the number one, is <u>always</u> typed as a word.

Example: There is only one boy to be recommended for a prize.

It is typed as a figure within dates, addresses or business documents.

Examples: 1st, 14th, 21st; Invoice No. 1; Your order No. 114, etc.

All other numbers are acceptable as figures, except at the beginning

of a sentence. (See line 2, Exercise V.)

The sign @ (meaning at) is used in business documents <u>only</u>.

The * is used to mark a reference within a text which is then

referred to in a footnote.

2. Check your work. If it is inaccurate, practise any lines/words you found to be difficult and then type a further copy to keep for reference. If accurate, type it once more, trying to speed up on figures.

LESSON 21

ACCURACY/SPEED BUILDING

1. Proceed as for previous accuracy/speed building exercises, using a 1 inch (25 mm) left-hand margin and single-line spacing.

Exercise I

Inspiration will come after accomplishing the skill of typewriting.

John has little time for Jane who only enjoys jewellery making.

Keep Karen happy by showing her kindness during this difficult time.

Like many lonely people, Luke loves regular visitors.

The water-based fluid is best — the chemical-based fluids thicken and need thinners added from time to time.

The neatest corrections are made with an eraser (typewriting rubber). In a later lesson you will be taught how to correct using an eraser.

4. Repeat Exercise III using, where necessary, either correction strip or the automatic correction facility found on some electric and all electronic machines. You should 'feel' when you make an error and stop to correct it. Do not remove the paper from the machine until you have checked that you have corrected all the errors.

COMPOSING AT THE MACHINE

In previous lessons you have been copying from printed script or manuscript, but in future you may wish to put your thoughts directly in to typescript rather than writing them out and then typing from manuscript. When composing at the machine, you should look at the words as they appear on your typing paper. **Don't be tempted to look at the keys or you will 'undo' all the hard work you have put into learning to touch-type.**

1. Read once again the information you typed in Exercise III.
2. Retype, in your own words, any of the information that you can remember. Do not stop to correct errors.
3. Type two paragraphs giving your views on your present typing ability. **Remember to keep your eyes on the words as they appear on the typing paper.**

As you will see, it is much more difficult to compose **accurately** at the machine than it is to type from printed script, but with practice you will soon be able to put your thoughts directly on to the machine.

Note: In future exercises use correction strip/automatic correction facility **only** when instructed to do so.

LESSON 26

HANGING PARAGRAPHS

1. Study the hanging paragraphs below (Exercise I). As you will see, the first line is typed at the margin and all subsequent lines indented **two** spaces.

Figure 29

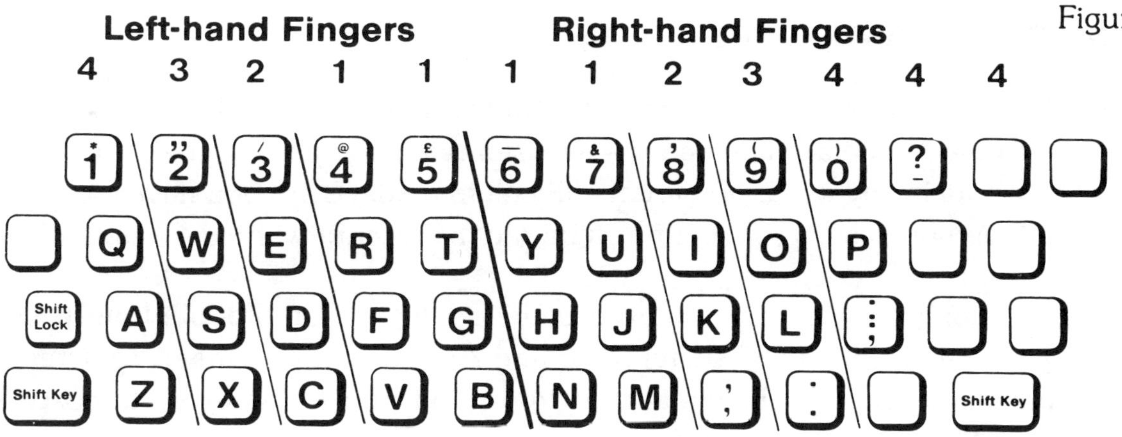

NEW KEYS — Figures 3, 5 and 7 (upper case characters / £ and &)

1. Locate the figures 3, 5 and 7 and practise finger movements.
2. Keeping your eyes on the copy and paying attention to rhythmic movements, type the following exercises **once** only.

Exercise II

```
de3 de3 de3 de3 de3 de3 de3 de3 de/ de/ de/ de/ de/ de/ de/ de/

d3d d3d d3d d3d d3d d3d d3d d3d d/d d/d d/d d/d d/d d/d d/d d/d
```

Exercise III

```
fr5 fr5 fr5 fr5 fr5 fr5 fr5 fr5 fr£ fr£ fr£ fr£ fr£ fr£ fr£ fr£

f5f f5f f5f f5f f5f f5f f5f f5f f£f f£f f£f f£f f£f f£f f£f f£f
```

Exercise IV

```
ju7 ju7 ju7 ju7 ju7 ju7 ju7 ju7 ju& ju& ju& ju& ju& ju& ju& ju&

j7j j7j j7j j7j j7j j7j j7j j7j j&j j&j j&j j&j j&j j&j j&j j&j
```

Exercise V

```
Pages 3/5 refer to the year 1973.  Pages 5/7 refer to the year 1975.

John Lamb & Co. Ltd., 53 & 55, Long Lane, Bexley, Kent.

They can supply new books at £3.50 each.  Please order 37 copies.
```

3. Check Exercise V. Carry out improvement practice where necessary.
4. Type the exercise once more.

Note: The ampersand (&) is used in names and addresses only. (See line 2, Exercise V.) It is not used in ordinary matter.

TYPING FROM MANUSCRIPT

Before attempting to type from a manuscript not written by yourself, read it through carefully. This will enable you to become accustomed to the writing, check on difficult spelling and write in any words you found difficult to read. Once you have completed the preparation you will be confident to type the manuscript without hesitation.

1. Read and prepare the following exercise before typing it in **double-line** spacing, using margins of 25 and 85 (Elite) or 15 and 75 (Pica). **Remember: to listen for the margin warning bell; make the right-hand margin as even as possible.** (Refer to Line-end Division, Lesson 22.)

Exercise II

If you expect your work to be considered for
publication, or an essay or assignment you are
submitting to a tutor to receive a good mark,
make sure it is beautifully presented. All
human beings are influenced by first impressions!

2. Check your work, paying special attention to line-ends.
3. Using A5 paper with the long edge at the top (landscape), type one copy of the following exercise. Use blocked paragraphs, single-line spacing, a left margin of 1½ inches (38 mm) and a right margin of 1 inch (25 mm). **Remember to read and prepare the exercise before you type it.**

Exercise III

(N.B. The information given below refers to machines without an automatic correction facility.)

If you make an error, NEVER back-
space and type the correct letter over the
incorrect one. The quickest method of
correcting mistakes is to. use a correcting
strip.

Correcting fluid is also available for
painting out words/sections to be altered.

continued over

CONSOLIDATION

1. Type the following exercise **once** only, keeping your eyes on the copy throughout.

Exercise VI

Were you born between 1935 and 1940?

Eighteen children will be accompanying us to Lucerne.

There will be 11 boys and 7 girls present.

John's address is 35a, The Parade, Cowes, Isle of Wight.

The fare to London is £17.50 for adults; £10.25 for children.

Please arrive at 3.45 p.m. We will begin at four o'clock.

The party is on 6th May at 8 p.m. Mr. & Mrs. Harris are expected.

2. Check your work and carry out improvement practice where necessary.
3. Read the following exercise and then type a copy to keep for reference.

Exercise VII

Note that in line 6 of the above exercise the <u>word</u> four replaced <u>figure</u> 4 when followed by o'clock. Figures are always used before the abbreviations a.m. and p.m. No full stop is required when using 24-hour clock times. For example, we type 3.45 p.m. or 1545 hrs; 11.30 a.m. or 1130 hours. The word hours, or its abbreviation, is sometimes eliminated.

4. Check your work paying particular attention to correct spacing after punctuation. If you have made errors in spacing or typed incorrect figures, carry out improvement practice.

3. Type the following exercise, **once** only, using double-line spacing and margins of 25 and 85 or 15 and 75. Note that the 'superior' characters (line 3) are typed a half-space **above** the line and the 'inferior' characters (line 4) a half-space **below** the line, by turning the cylinder back or forward a half-space. **Remember to return to the original line of type before proceeding to type the next character.**

Exercise IV

The trip will cost over $850 per person. Help! Fire!

30 x 5 = 150; 24 ÷ 4 = 6; 16 x 5 = 80; Attention!

The oven should be set on 400 ^{o}F or 200 ^{o}C (Regulo 6).

The lowered figures in H_2O and CO_2 are 'inferior' characters.

4. Check your work. If time allows, type the exercise once more.

PREPARATION

For Lesson 26 you will need A6 size paper (approx. envelope size). Cut 2 sheets of A4 in half (A5) and then in half again (A6).

For Lesson 27 you will need:

Four sheets of A5 paper.

One sheet of A5 carbon paper.

Two sheets of A5 bank (flimsy copy paper).

Manual users only:
One hard typewriting rubber and a soft rubber. (If you need to buy a typing eraser, choose the round (or hexagonal) variety. The softer, 'pencil-type' typewriting eraser is better for carbon copy correction than top copy correction.)

LESSON 25

ACCURACY/SPEED BUILDING

1. Proceed as for previous accuracy/speed building exercises, using a 1 inch (25 mm) left margin and single-line spacing.

Exercise I

Wax polish, plus hard work, makes dull wood shine once more.

Xmas is the time for exhibiting presents expertly boxed and wrapped.

Youth should be enjoyed as it very quickly passes.

Zones for parking are few in this hazardous city maze.

LESSON 22

ACCURACY/SPEED BUILDING

1. Proceed as for previous accuracy/speed building exercises, using a 1 inch (25 mm) left margin and single-line spacing.

Exercise I

Most men manage their own monthly meeting arrangements.

Names and their origins can be a fascinating study.

One day the owner of the flat she occupies will return home.

Paragraphs typed in block appear to be preferable to most typists.

BLOCKED PARAGRAPHS

1. Set the margin stops at 24 and 88 (Elite) or 10 and 74 (Pica).
2. Read the following paragraphs before typing them once, **exactly as shown,** in single-line spacing, leaving one line-space between each paragraph.

Exercise II

When typing paragraphs in single-line spacing, one clear line-
space must be left between each paragraph.

Since commencing to type you have been practising paragraph
spacing by leaving one line-space between each set of three
lines you typed.

A typist may use blocked, indented or hanging paragraphs,
depending on the requirements of the piece of work she has
to type. The paragraphs shown in this exercise are blocked
paragraphs - each line begins at the margin. These are the
most commonly used. (Indented and hanging paragraphs will be
dealt with in a later lesson.)

2. Check your work. If you have more than 3 errors, or have not left the correct spacing between paragraphs, retype the exercise.

3. Pin a copy of the above exercise to the exercise you typed yesterday (Exercise IV) and before you file them, study the differences between indented and blocked paragraphs typed in **double-line** spacing.

COMBINATION CHARACTERS

When a character, such as an asterisk, does not appear on a machine as a single character, it can be made up by combining two characters.

1. Locate the mechanisms that are used to position these characters:

   Back-space (key) – positioned on right or left of keyboard, probably marked with an arrow.

   Interliner (lever) – positioned on right or left of the carriage. (Some machines do not include this mechanism.)

2. Practise the following combination characters for those characters that do not appear on your keyboard.

   * (asterisk) – Type x, depress and release the back-space key once and type a hyphen (-).

   ! (exclamation mark) – Type apostrophe ('), back-space and type a full stop.

   ÷ (division sign) – Type a colon (:), back-space and type a hyphen.

   = (equation sign) – Type a hyphen, back-space and type a second hyphen a little above the first by **either:**

   (a) pulling forward the interliner to release the ratchet before turning the cylinder gently **towards** you and typing a second hyphen. (By replacing the interliner and turning the cylinder **away** from you the machine will automatically return to the original line of type.) **or:**

   (b) using the variable line-spacer to move slightly above the original line of type before typing the second hyphen. (This mechanism will not return automatically to the original line of type – your eye will tell you when you are back in position.)

   $ (dollar sign) – Type a capital S, back-space and type a solidus (/).

   † (dagger) – Type a capital I, back-space and type a hyphen.

   ‡ (double dagger) – Type a capital I, back-space and type an equation sign (or two hyphens).

Note: When daggers, double-daggers and asterisks are used within a text, they are typed a half-space above the line of type, but when used in a footnote, may be typed in the normal position.

LINE-END DIVISION

You will have noticed that both left and right-hand margin stops were set for the above exercise and that the margin warning bell rang each time you neared the end of the typing line. The purpose of the bell was to warn you that you were coming to the margin stop. For Exercise II you were given the correct margin stops to use in order to type the lines to begin and end **exactly** as printed. In future, you will have to type from printed copy of varying lengths where lines could be shorter or longer than your paper or chosen typing line. Sometimes you will be typing from manuscript which gives little indication of the length of line. A good typist keeps the length of line and the right-hand margin as even as possible by listening for the warning bell and quickly deciding whether the next word should be started and finished on the present line, hyphenated, or carried to the following line. The basic rules for line-end division are as follows:

1. **Divide:**	**Examples:**
After prefix or before suffix	dis-agree, play-ing
According to syllables	prac-tise
Between double consonants	drum-mer
Words already hyphenated – **at the hyphen only**	line-end

2. **Do Not Divide:**	
Words of one syllable (or their plurals)	fox, foxes
Where only two letters would be taken to the second line	painted (not paint-ed)
Proper names (including courtesy titles) or abbreviations	Winchester, Mr. Jones, B.B.C.
Sums of money	£246.50

3. Avoid division where possible and **never** divide the last word of a paragraph or page or on more than 2 consecutive lines. (When in doubt as to the correct point of division, consult a dictionary.)

MARGIN WARNING BELL

The number of character spaces left after the warning bell sounds – before the margin stop is reached – varies with makes of machine.

1. To establish the number of spaces on your machine, practise the following:
   a) Take the printing point to 70 (Elite) or 60 (Pica).
   b) Tap the space bar until the bell rings/bleeps.
   c) Continue tapping the space bar, counting the number of spaces before the carriage/carrier stops. **Leave the carriage/carrier at the margin stop.**

Exercise II

A good typist takes care of her typewriter by covering it at the end of the day, cleaning it when necessary and making sure that it is always in a safe position when not in use.

2. Check your work.
3. If you did not finish within the target time, type it once more.

BLOCKED PARAGRAPHS TYPED IN DOUBLE-LINE SPACING

When **blocked** paragraphs are typed in **double-line** spacing, an extra space is left between the paragraphs (i.e. return the carriage/carrier and turn up one more line, as for all paragraphs in single-line spacing).

1. Type the following exercise on A4 paper in **double-line** spacing, using margins of 25 and 88 (Elite) or 15 and 78 (Pica).

Exercise III

There are three different forms of paragraphing. You have practised blocked and indented paragraphs and later you will practise hanging paragraphs.

Hanging paragraphs are sometimes used in display work and also in documents such as specifications.

In business letters blocked paragraphs are the most commonly used, although some firms still prefer to use indented paragraphs.

Indented paragraphs are preferable for literary work or other work where double-line spacing is required, as the number of words on a page are more easily calculated and much less paper is used than for blocked paragraphs.

As this exercise shows, it is necessary to leave space between blocked paragraphs to enable the reader to see exactly where each paragraph begins and ends.

MARGIN RELEASE KEY

By depressing and releasing the MARGIN RELEASE KEY (usually placed on the right of the keyboard) the typist is able to type beyond the set margin stop in order to complete a word. When the carriage is returned, the margin stop is automatically locked into its normal set position.

1. Locate the margin release and practise the following:
   a) Using the little finger, depress and release the key.
   b) Tap the space bar or keys to take the carriage/carrier into the right margin.
   c) Return carriage/carrier.

CONSOLIDATION

1. Study the examples of correct line-end division shown in Exercise III and then type each line **three** times. **Remember to leave one line space between each set of three lines.**

Exercise III

```
chil-dren, dis-agree, prac-tice, neces-sity, line-end, direc-tion

test-ing, suf-fix, junc-tion, self-evident, com-plete, re-enter.
```

2. Type Exercise II once more, using margin stops of 30 and 80 (Elite) or 20 and 70 (Pica). Try to keep the right-hand margin even by listening for the margin warning bell and deciding whether it will be best to complete or divide words at line-ends. **Remember to use the margin release when it is necessary to type past the margin stop in order to complete a word.**
3. Check your work. Have you divided words according to the rules? Is your right margin as even as the first typing of the exercise?
4. If time allows, type the exercise once more. **Remember to keep your eyes on the copy throughout.**
5. Select your best attempt to keep for reference.

PREPARATION (Manual machine users only.)

For Lesson 25 you will need chemical correcting strip (correction paper). Small packets of correction paper are available from most stationery shops or chain-store stationery counters.

8. The following exercise is to be typed in **double-line** spacing, using margins of 20 and 85 (Elite) or 12 and 77 (Pica). As you will see, no extra space is left between **indented** paragraphs when typed in **double-line** spacing. **Remember to: indent the first line of each paragraph; keep your eyes on the copy.**

Exercise IV

Sometimes I would arrive when chicks were actually hatching. I loved to watch this and was fascinated that the eggs could, in fact, be hatched under the warmth of a lamp without the aid of a hen.

Being engrossed with the chicks and Max, I would often become unconscious of time and the fact that my mother was probably waiting for the eggs for tea. When I eventually remembered the real reason for being there I would reluctantly leave the old man and the chicks and hurry home with my basket of fresh brown eggs.

9. Check your work. Did you indent **both** paragraphs? Did you remember not to turn up an extra space between paragraphs?
10. If time allows, type the exercise once more.

LESSON 24

ACCURACY/SPEED BUILDING

1. Proceed as for previous accuracy/speed building exercises, using a 1½ inch (38 mm) left margin and single-line spacing.

Exercise I

Twenty students will attend the meeting.

Umbrellas are seldom used as sunshades.

Visitors to Venice spend their vacation viewing and walking.

SPEED TEST (Target time: 1½ minutes – Errors allowed: one)

1. Using margins of 25 and 87 (Elite) or 16 and 78 (Pica), type the following exercise once for practice and then once at speed. **Remember to: prepare to type with care; keep your eyes on the copy throughout; return the carriage/carrier promptly; keep your wrists and fingers loose.**

LESSON 23

ACCURACY/SPEED BUILDING

1. Proceed as for previous accuracy/speed building exercises, but this time type each **paragraph** three times. Use margins of 20 and 85 (Elite) or 10 and 75 (Pica) and single-line spacing. **Remember to leave a clear line-space between paragraphs.**

Exercise I

```
Quiet people quite often need to be questioned before they quote
their views.

Regular visits to the cross roads proved that a roundabout was
required in order to keep the traffic flowing.

Severe shock is often followed by shaking and sweating of the
body.
```

THE TABULATOR

The tabulator is a device for moving the carriage/carrier to a pre-determined position.

1. Check whether your typewriter has a tabulator **key** or **bar.** If the tabulator key is to the right or left of the keyboard, the appropriate little finger should be used for its operation. If your machine has a tabulator **bar** above the keyboard, the first finger of the right hand should be used.
2. Also check whether your machine has a tabulator **set** key (marked +) and a tabulator **clear** key (marked -). (Some typewriters have a pre-set mechanism which means that when the tabulator key/bar is depressed, the carriage will move only to the pre-set points shown on the paper scale — in this case there will be no **set** or **clear** keys on the machine.)
3. To clear any tab points previously set on your machine, carry out the following routine:
   a) Depress the tabulator key/bar to allow the carriage/carrier to travel freely.
   b) If the carriage/carrier stops at any point, clear the tabulator stop by depressing the **clear** key once.
   c) Continue to depress the tabulator key/bar followed by the **clear** key at the points at which the carriage stops.

Note: If you have the **pre-set** type of tabulator you will not be able to set tab stops at chosen points and you must therefore use the first pre-set tab point (from the left-hand margin) when typing the following exercises.

INDENTED PARAGRAPHS

The following paragraphs (Exercises II and III) are called 'indented' paragraphs — the first line being indented five spaces from the margin.

1. Prepare to type the exercises by setting margins at 20 and 80 (Elite) or 12 and 72 (Pica). From the left margin, tap five spaces on the space bar and depress and release the tabulator **set** key.

2. Check that you have set the tabulator stop at the correct point on the scale by returning the carriage and depressing the tabulator key/bar. If it is correctly set, the carriage will stop with the printing point at 25 (Elite) or 17 (Pica). If it is incorrectly set, depress the **clear** key, check that your paper is inserted at '0' on the paper scale and that your margins are correctly set and then tap five spaces from the margin and re-set the tabulator stop.

3. Practise depressing the tabulator key/bar and returning to the home keys without looking at the keyboard. When you are able to do this, type the following paragraphs in single-line spacing on A4 paper. **Remember to: leave one clear line-space between each paragraph; press the tabulator at the beginning of each paragraph; keep your eyes on the copy.**

Exercise II

```
     Scissors and coloured paper - sometimes even newspaper -
can amuse a small child for many hours.

     Children also like to stick pieces of paper together
using paste made from flour and water.
```

4. Repeat the above paragraphs until you are 'indenting' with ease.

5. Type the following exercise **once** only.

Exercise III

```
     There are, so far, only 6 boys and 9 girls interested
in the trip to the Tower of London.  We need at least 8 more
to make the visit worth-while.

     If you know of children in any other group who may be
interested in the trip, please inform them that this will
take place on 29th May.  I must have final numbers by
12th May.
```

6. Check your work. Carry out improvement practice where necessary.

7. Type the exercise once more.